SUPERMARINE ATTACKER, SWIFT AND SCIMITAR

A production Attacker F1, WA497, with the familiar background of the Needles off the Isle of Wight. *Vickers*

SUPERMARINE
SWIFT AND

PHILIP BIRTLES

ATTACKER,
SCIMITAR

Publishing

Contents

First published 1992

ISBN 0 7110 2034 5

Published by Ian Allan Ltd, Shepperton, Surrey; and printed by Ian Allan Printing Ltd at their works at Coombelands in Runnymede, England

Line drawings by M. A. (Tony) Burns.

Front cover:
A trio of FAA Supermarine Attackers in formation.

Rear cover top:
Swift FRS XD953:F of No 79 Squadron, RAF Germany. *MoD*

Rear cover bottom:
Scimitar F1, XD264:154/V of 803 Squadron, aboard HMS *Victorious*.
RAF Museum/Cyril Peach

Previous page:
Swift FR5 on a production test flight. *M. J. F. Bowyer*

Foreword

This book is about three jet fighters of the fifties; a decade unique in the history of aeronautical development when the rate of change was faster than it had ever been before or has been since.

In the 1950s the SBAC Show at Farnborough was an annual event and was opened to the public for the first time. They were rewarded every year with a display of new types of aircraft and engines in 'flying test beds'. Until the Royal Air Force Aerobatic Team was reformed there was no service participation; the Industry had quite enough to make a great show and it was all British.

This was the time when the latest prototypes took part in air races, when records for absolute speed and altitude were established, also closed circuit and inter city records. In the early fifties the potential seemed unlimited but if the decade started with a roar it ended with a whimper after the Government White Paper on Defence in 1957 proclaimed the end of development of 'Manned Fighter Aircraft'.

All this was around 40 years ago and, as anyone who has tried to preserve records will tell you, the passage of time and the passing of people involved makes the task difficult and often thankless, which is surprising in view of the great interest there is in historical as well as contemporary aviation. So books like this one are important because they preserve the records as well as making it easier to study them.

Philip Birtles has assembled a substantial quantity of detail and has presented it very clearly. You will learn a great deal about these three aircraft and the prototypes from which they were developed. You will also read about the aircraft which might have followed them had these projects not been cancelled. Perhaps you will reflect on what it meant to the future of the Industry and the flying services.

The fighter version of the Swift was also cancelled and branded a failure. This was more a matter of political expediency than technical fact because even the F1 was a great advance on what was in service. It was the events of the day from which the Swift suffered. It was too late for the Korean War and it was the first of its kind to reach the service; everybody was learning. The standard of the fighter pilots wanted was manifest in the North American F-86, the Sabre. This was indeed the Spitfire of the early fifties and like the Spitfire had some unusual handling qualities which

pilots were prepared to put up with because of its outstanding performance and manoeuvrability. They also liked the cockpit systems and the engineers liked the ease of maintenance. However, it must be said, that all these features benefited from not having to comply with British technical requirements.

Politics began to play an increasingly important part in the development of aircraft during the fifties. During the sixties the Government of the day succeeded in cancelling the most significant military project every undertaken in Britain, the TSR2, in order to release funds for the Party programme. This book is not about politics – it would be much thicker if it was – but let me mention two points which link the beginning and the end of the story and, perhaps, show us what might have been.

In the first chapter we read about the Spitfire: 'Mitchell's aim was to produce the most compact and cleanest design around the Rolls-Royce engine and a pilot, while retaining the armament of the eight machine guns'.

And in the final chapter, about the submission to GOR 339 (which became TSR2): 'The Supermarine Design team favoured the lower weight, single engined project. Their reasoning was that powerplant unreliability was more likely to be caused by ancillaries rather than the basic engine and by providing duplication of the engine systems a great deal could be saved in terms of cost of developing and operating the aircraft'.

It was the brilliant submission of the Supermarine team which got Vickers chosen to partner English Electric in the development of TSR2. The customer decided to have two engines. The last of the line which can be traced back through the aircraft described in this book to the Spitfire and the Schneider Trophy winners can be seen at Duxford where it has been beautifully restored by the Imperial War Museum. When you look at it remember that had it not been cancelled 25 years ago, Tornado pilots of today could be flying an aircraft their fathers had flown; and they would find it had all the capability of what they fly now, and then some.

David Morgan   *December 1991*
Buckfastleigh

Introduction

The story of the Supermarine jet fighters appeared to be a much neglected subject as far as recording their history and development was concerned. This may have been due to the poor performance of the early Swifts, which was more than made up for by the later marks. During the research and development of these aircraft, a considerable pioneering spirit became apparent, pushing forward the unknown boundaries of transonic flight research within a low budget and achieving eventually a high degree of success in terms of reliability and performance. It was unfortunate that larger numbers were not required to make the programmes more profitable.

In compiling this book I should like to thank David Morgan for his firsthand knowledge of the test flying and much of the significant design activity. For photographic selections, I would like to thank Michael Bowyer, John Rawlings, Mike Gradidge, Maurice Marsh, Tom Crossett and Alan Fisher for searching through their photo collections to give a broad coverage of previously unpublished pictures. Also, I would like to thank Andrew Renwick of the RAF Museum, David Richardson of the FAA Museum and Brian Wexham of Vickers Plc for assistance in obtaining some of the official photographs from their archives.

Finally, I should like to thank Tyler Parris and my wife, Martha, for their major contributions in putting my handwritten script into the word processor.

Philip J. Birtles
Stevenage, May 1991

Right:
No 800 (B) Squadron Scimitar F1, XD321:116/E, is pictured flying from Lossiemouth in August 1965.
J. D. R. Rawlings

1
Vickers Supermarine

Undoubtedly best known for the fine World War 2 Spitfire, Supermarine had a long pioneering history from the earliest days of aviation, right through to the jet age with all the challenges of breaking the sound barrier.

It was in October 1913 that Noel Pemberton Billing registered the name Supermarine as his telegraphic address, the aim being to build a flying boat. His start in aviation was in 1904 when he built a man-lifting glider and he gained his Royal Aero Club Certificate as a qualified pilot in 1912.

His first design was the Supermarine PB1 flying boat with a single tractor engine mounted between biplane wings on a cigar shaped hull. Despite the advanced concept of the design, it failed to fly.

The company was formally registered on 27 June 1914 with its factory next to the Woolston Ferry on the River Itchen at Southampton.

At the outbreak of World War 1, Pemberton Billing decided to produce a single-seat fighter which was designed and built in the incredibly short time of nine days, officially known as the PB9. The speed of production was assisted by the purchase of an existing set of wings, and attaching them to a braced mortice and tenon-jointed fuselage which could be made by any competent cabinet maker, to give rapid production. This aircraft flew successfully on 12 August 1914, but was not ordered into production.

Towards the end of 1916 the organisation was named The Supermarine Aviation Works Ltd, with Hubert Scott-Paine as the managing director. Also in 1916, Reginald Mitchell joined the company, later to become the designer of the Schneider Trophy winners and the immortal Spitfire. The major duties during World War 1 were aircraft repair and experimental work for the Admiralty, and the design of single-seat pusher propeller scout aircraft. Supermarine's most successful aircraft of World War 1 was the N1B Baby,

Below:
The advanced-looking Pemberton Billing PB1 flying boat exhibited at the 1914 Olympia Aero Show. Unfortunately it failed to fly! *Vickers*

Below:
The rather unattractive PB31E Night Hawk, 1388, designed to defend Britain against the Zeppelins. *RAF Museum*

Bottom:
Pemberton Billing's most successful aircraft of World War 1 was the N1b Baby N59. *RAF Museum*

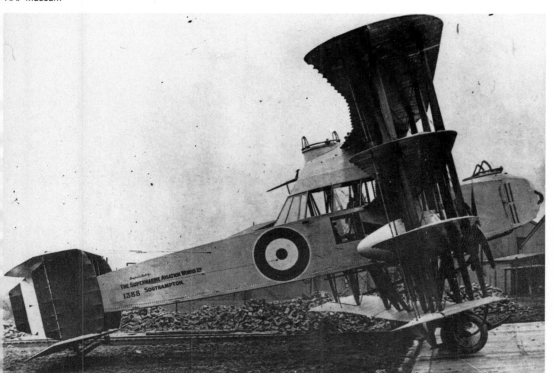

a pusher flying-boat, but the war ended before it was able to enter service.

In the difficult years of economic hardship following the postwar slump in aviation in 1919, Supermarine produced a new three-passenger commercial flying boat known as the Channel Type, which was sold in South and Central America, Norway, Japan and Britain.

The company then began to evolve its expertise in four different areas of aircraft development. These were basic single-engined amphibians; larger passenger-carrying flying-boats; Schneider Trophy monoplane racing seaplanes; and finally single-seat, single-engined fighters culminating in the Spitfire.

Designs of the general purpose single-engined amphibians started with the Seagull of the 1920s and finished with the advanced variable incidence wing Seagull air/sea rescue aircraft of 1948. The classic flying boats started with the twin-engined Southampton of 1925 and ended with the Stranraer of 1936. The Schneider Trophy experience commenced as early as

Top left:

The Air Yacht, G-AASE, was Supermarine's first multi-engined monoplane, ordered as a luxury transport by the Hon A. E. Guinness. *RAF Museum*

Centre left:

Seagull Vs for the RAAF were similar to the classic Walrus used widely for air/sea rescue and reconnaissance duties by the RAF. *RAF Museum*

Bottom left:

The ultimate Supermarine flying boat was the Seagull ASR1 advanced fleet reconnaissance amphibian. Only two prototypes were completed and PA147 was the second. *Vickers*

Right:

Designed by R. J. Mitchell, the Southampton was the first of the larger series of Supermarine flying boats. Southampton I, S1043, had a wooden hull and was powered by a pair of Napier Lion engines. *RAF Museum*

Below:

Southampton IV, S1648, became the prototype Scapa, powered by a pair of Rolls-Royce Kestrel engines, and was of all-metal construction. *Vickers*

Above:
The Stranraer was Supermarine's last twin-engined flying boat. *Vickers*

1919 when the Sea Lion 1 single-engined pusher biplane flying boat was entered, but the monoplane racing seaplanes did not participate in the competition until after 1925. This series of major international competitions was fought over primarily by Britain, the USA and Italy as well as a number of other nations. Britain eventually became the outright winner in 1931 with the Supermarine S6B by winning over three consecutive years.

The designer of these high performance single-engined seaplanes was Reginald Mitchell, building up experience from which he eventually created the Spitfire. In the early years, Supermarine had sponsored its own entry in the Schneider Trophy, but in 1927 the British Government supported the event by ordering seven special high-speed racing seaplanes for the RAF's High Speed Flight. Three of these were Supermarine S5s, one of them winning the trophy that year at an average speed of 281.65mph.

Late in 1928, Vickers (Aviation) Ltd acquired the Supermarine Aviation Works, becoming Vickers Supermarine Ltd. In 1929 Rolls-Royce developed the new 'R' engine which achieved 1,900hp; Mitchell incorporated it into the S5 development known as the S6. In 1929 the S6 beat the Italian entry in the Schneider contest at a speed of 328.63mph.

If Britain won the 1931 Schneider Trophy race, the trophy would be theirs to keep outright. However, the government unaccountably withdrew its support. Supermarine was unable to provide the finance but, at the eleventh hour, Lady Houston stepped into the arena and offered the considerable sum of £100,000 to cover the costs of building a new aircraft and entering

Below:
Amongst a number of single-engined amphibians, the Sea Lion III, N170, was flown in the 1923 Schneider Trophy race at Cowes. *RAF Museum*

a British team. With only six months to go, the Supermarine S6B powered by an improved Rolls-Royce engine developing 2,300hp for a short period, was supplied. In the event the Italians, who were the main challenge, were unable to participate, allowing Britain to fly the course solo at an average speed of 340.08mph to retain the Trophy for all time. Later the S6B achieved a new world speed record of 407.5mph.

During this period, flying boat development had continued, including the adoption by the RAF of the Scapa.

Above:
For the 1929 Schneider Trophy race Supermarine produced the S6, similar to the S5, but of all-metal construction. It was also powered by the new Rolls-Royce R engine. N247 at Woolston was the first of two ordered by the Air Ministry. This aircraft was flown to victory against the Italians by Flg Off H. R. D. Waghorn at a speed of 328.63mph. *Vickers*

Right:
The ultimate Supermarine Schneider Trophy design was the S6B, S1595, sponsored by Lady Houston, which was flown to victory in 1931 by Flt Lt J. N. Boothman, winning the Trophy outright for Britain.
RAF Museum

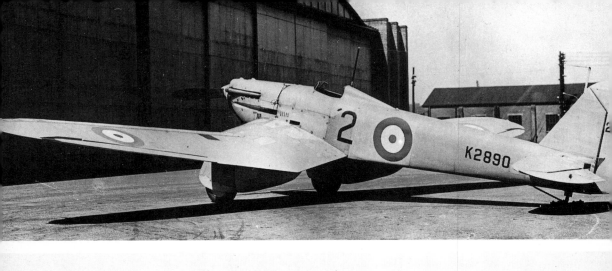

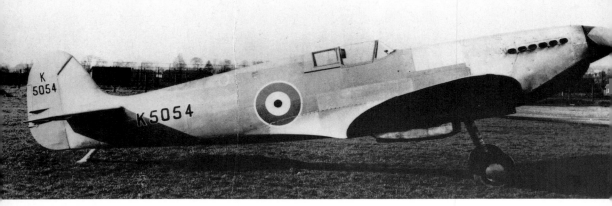

The roots of the Spitfire began in 1934 with a fairly basic single-seat aircraft to an unimaginative Specification F.7/30. Powered by a steam-cooled Goshawk engine, top speed was only 228mph, additional drag being generated by the fixed faired undercarriage. Supermarine therefore set out to design its own private venture fighter which – combined with the availability of the Rolls-Royce PV12 engine expected to develop 1,000hp, and the new Air Ministry Specification F.5/34 calling for an eight-gun fighter – resulted in the world-beating Spitfire. Mitchell's aim was to produce the most compact and cleanest design around the Rolls-Royce engine and a pilot, while retaining an armament of eight machine guns in the wings. The wing was a totally new elliptical planform with a thin section giving a fast, deadly, but docile combat aircraft. The main disadvantage of this classic wing was the difficulty of production.

Construction of the prototype proceeded rapidly at Eastleigh Airport near Southampton, and the aircraft is reported to have made its first flight in the hands of Mutt Summers on 5 March 1936. Having conceived this remarkable aircraft, its creator, Reginald Mitchell

Top:
The Supermarine F7/30 Type 224 prototype, K2890, which was completely redesigned by Mitchell to become the Spitfire. *RAF Museum*

Above:
Spitfire prototype, K5054, at Eastleigh, the first of over 22,000 Spitfires running to 33 different versions. *RAF Museum*

died of cancer the following year at the age of 42. The responsibility as chief designer was taken over by Joe Smith, who led the Supermarine design team throughout World War 2 and into the jet age with a whole range of Spitfire developments. The Spitfire was the only combat aircraft to be in production from the beginning to the end of World War 2, although its progressive development led to many changes, giving the aircraft only a superficial resemblance to its prewar origins. One of the major changes was the substitution of the Rolls-Royce Griffon engine for the Merlin at about halfway through its operational life. The cockpit canopy was also changed to the bubble type to improve all-round visibility.

Above:
Early Spitfire developments in the Hursley Park experimental hangar. *Vickers*

Right:
The splendid Hursley Park design and administrative offices used by Supermarine after enemy action had driven them from Woolston. *Vickers*

Below:
Spitfire Mk VBs in production at Castle Bromwich.
Vickers

The Spitfire entered service with No 19 Squadron at Duxford in 1938 and in 1939 production was building up not only at the home factory, but also at a new shadow factory at Castle Bromwich near Birmingham. Spitfire Is and IIs played a major part in the Battle of Britain alongside the numerically superior Hawker Hurricanes. The experience of trying to destroy the armour protected German aircraft, resulted in four of the Spitfire machine guns being replaced by a pair of the more destructive 20mm cannons.

The Supermarine Woolston Works were bombed in September 1940 resulting in the design team and headquarters staff moving to Hursley Park, a country house near Winchester, where they remained into the jet age. Production was also widely dispersed, reaching over 60 sites by 1944.

As well as being a day fighter, unarmed Spitfires were used for photo reconnaissance. Some had the wingtips clipped for better low-level performance, while others had them extended and a pressure cabin was added for high altitude interceptions. Following the experience of the Battle of Britain, the Spitfire Mk V was produced, but one of the most successful versions was the Mk IX powered by a two-stage supercharged Merlin 61 engine. This gave a top speed of just over 400mph. The Spitfire Mk XII was the first to be powered by the 2,000hp Griffon engine, but other variants still appeared with the Merlin engine. The Mk XIX was the major Griffon-powered photo reconnaissance Spitfire, three of which are preserved in flying condition with the Battle of Britain Memorial Flight. The Mk 21, 22 and 24 were the ultimate versions of the Spitfire, powered by the 2,050hp Griffon engine, featuring larger, stronger wings and in some cases contra-rotating airscrews. The Seafire was developed for the Fleet Air Arm, but the closely placed relatively fragile undercarriage was not ideal for deck operations.

From 1936 to 1945 the Spitfire's top speed had increased from 350mph to 450mph, bringing the aircraft close to the compressibility problems of transonic flight associated with the jet age pioneers. A total of 20,351 Spitfires were built, in addition to 2,408 Seafires for the Fleet Air Arm.

Supermarine was now on the threshold of the jet age, with all the challenges and unknowns which that was to bring.

Left:
The classic Spitfire: Mk II P7350 was restored for the film *Battle of Britain* **and is now a part of the RAF's Battle of Britain Memorial Flight.** *P. J. Birtles*

Top:
Later versions of the Spitfire had the Merlin engine replaced by the more powerful Rolls-Royce Griffon. PRXIX PS853 now serves with the Battle of Britain Memorial Flight. *P. J. Birtles*

Above:
Two-seat Spitfire Mk VIII, G-AIDN, was named after R. J. Mitchell and attended an air day at South Marston in June 1967. *P. J. Birtles*

Left:
The Seafire XV powered by a Griffon engine was a navalised version of the Spitfire FXII for operations with the Fleet Air Arm. *Vickers*

2
Attacker Development

Supermarine had taken the development of piston-engined aircraft to the extreme with the ultimate Spitfire developments, known as the Spiteful for the RAF and the Seafang for the Fleet Air Arm. The major development with these aircraft was to design a laminar flow wing featuring a whole new aerodynamic profile with the greatest thickness located further aft of the section than the conventional wings then in use.

However, it was found in practice that the smoothness of the skin was critical, and that minute irregularities, surface roughness or even dead flies stuck to the surface, could destroy much of the improvement in drag characteristics.

Supermarine wrote its own Specification 470 to cover the design of the laminar flow wing, allocating Type No 371, which was eventually adopted to cover the complete Spiteful aircraft. The object of the specification was threefold: to produce a wing design to raise as much as possible the critical speed at which the increase of drag became serious due to a phenomenon known as compressibility, on reaching the speed of sound; to obtain a higher rate of roll than any existing fighter; and to improve performance by reducing the profile drag.

Extensive assistance was received from the National Physical Laboratory (NPL) in the development of the most suitable wing section, which was to achieve laminar flow as far back on the wing as possible, where interference from slipstream or projection such as gun barrels would be avoided. The maximum thickness was at about 42% of the chord with an aileron reversal speed of 850mph being aimed for. The familiar Spitfire wing shape was abandoned for a straight tapered leading and trailing edge design to ease production, with conventional two-spar construction. Wing area was reduced by 38.5sq ft to 210, and the weight was 200lb lighter than the wing on the Spitfire Mk 21. A gain in speed of some 55mph was estimated.

The Spiteful was notable for the high level of wind tunnel testing made by the RAE and NPL, much of this work concentrated on the wing performance. Tests up to Mach 0.82 included different wing setting and the evolution of perfectly smooth wing surface, even to the extent of considering a complete composite wing well ahead of its time.

Flight trials of the Spiteful highlighted a number of unsatisfactory features, such as aileron snatching, wing drop just prior to the stall and a pronounced flick at the stall under high gravity loadings, or 'g'. It soon became apparent that the Spiteful did not offer any significant advantages over the later Spitfires, but the new wing development appeared promising. The batch

Below:
The naval version of the Spiteful was the Seafang featuring a new fuselage and fitted with a laminar flow wing, later to be used on the Attacker.
RAF Museum

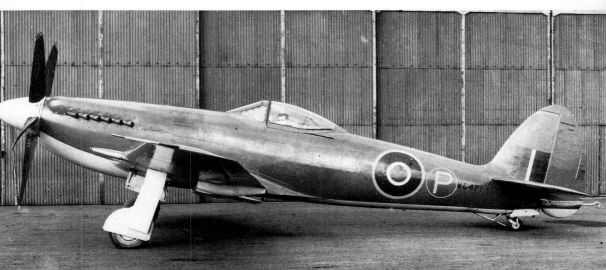

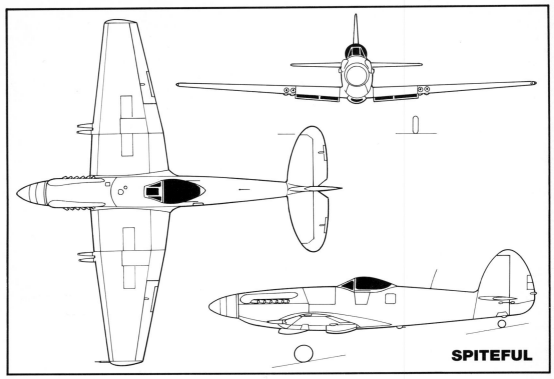

SPITEFUL

of 17 Spitefuls completed were therefore allocated to the improvement of the laminar flow wing in preparation for its use in a jet-propelled application. In these trials a level speed of 494mph was achieved, but the boosted Rolls-Royce Griffon engine suffered from the extreme treatment.

With the Spiteful failing to gain a service entry, Supermarine then looked at a naval development known as the Seafang. This aircraft featured the same basic wing, but with folding tips to allow storage aboard ship. This combination handled very well in deck trials and simulated landings at the test airfield of Chilbolton and RNAS Ford. Two Seafang prototypes were built, and 10 production aircraft out of an order for 150, before cancellation of the programme.

However, despite their cancellation, these two types contributed a considerable amount to transonic research leading neatly into the jet age.

A week before the first flight of the prototype Spiteful on 30 June 1944, Supermarine started the drawing for a jet propelled aircraft to the official specification E.10/44, the initial outline design being submitted to the Ministry of Aircraft Production as Supermarine Specification 477 only a week later.

With official approval, Rolls-Royce had started the design of a large jet engine in March 1944 with twice the thrust of existing turbojets available, including the Derwent engines for the Gloster Meteor. The new engine, designated the RB40, was to be capable of developing over 4,000lb static thrust, and it was this engine which Supermarine was asked to consider in its submission for E.10/44, making use of its laminar flow wing experience. However, Joe Smith, Supermarine Chief Designer, preferred a smaller engine and the turbojet was reduced in size to develop an anticipated 3,000lb thrust, re-designated the RB41 and eventually became the Nene as part of the family of Rolls-Royce jet engines named after British rivers.

The Supermarine design submitted featured a new fuselage containing the Nene engine, a forward-mounted pressurised cockpit, and the Type 371 laminar flow wings with additional fuel tanks replacing radiators. Fuel capacity was increased to 395gal and the four 20mm wing-mounted cannon armament was retained. Supermarine allocated Type No 392 to what was eventually to become the Attacker.

Initial flight trials of the RB41 engine were disappointing, but with minor modification the engine exceeded its original estimates, achieving 4,500lb thrust.

Following studies by the Ministry of Aircraft Production, it was realised that any problems with the laminar flow wings would be solved with the Spiteful prototypes. Supermarine was advised that three prototypes of the new jet aircraft would be required, and the order was placed on 5 August for three 'Jet machines of the Spiteful type', allocated identities TS409, 413, 416. The second and third aircraft were to have provi-

sion for naval operations. After official inspection of the partly completed mock-up, the first draft specification E.10/44 was issued, matching essentially the Supermarine Type 477.

Despite the early loss of the first Spiteful prototype and some problems with low speed characteristics, the Ministry supported the continuation of the programme and Treasury approval was obtained for a pre-production batch of 24 aircraft. Six of these aircraft were to the original E.10/44 specification and the remaining 18 were to a new E.1/45 naval requirement, the contract being issued on 21 November 1945.

Due to the handling difficulties with the Spiteful, first flight of the E.10/44 was delayed, and so in

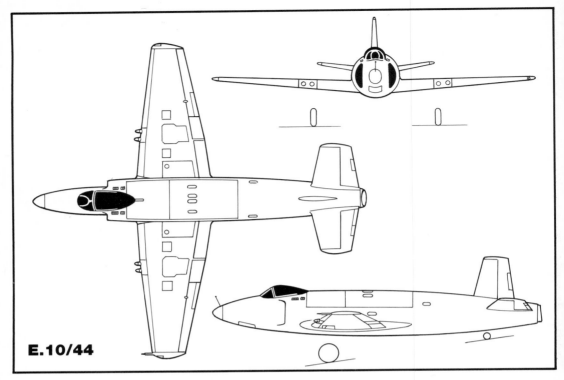

E.10/44

February 1946 the Admiralty asked for work on the naval version to be suspended, ordering 18 Sea Vampire F20s instead. The contract for the 24 pre-production aircraft was shelved for the time being, but work on the three prototypes was permitted to continue.

The aileron development caused major delays, with flight trials of the Spiteful revealing that the slotted aileron with geared balance tabs become too heavy at speeds of more than 400mph. It was therefore decided to reserve the second aircraft for development and investigation of the handling characteristics. This work at that time was on the threshold of knowledge of the approach to the speed of sound.

Flight trials with the Attacker commenced at Boscombe Down on 27 July with the maiden flight by Jeffrey Quill, Supermarine's Chief Test Pilot. Not only was the aircraft new, but it was the first to be powered by the new Nene engine, and the first prototype to be flight-tested from Boscombe Down. Initial flights were powered by Nene No 13 limited to 12,000rpm giving 4,300lb thrust. Later, however, a No 28 engine was fitted, raising the rpm to 12,440 delivering a thrust of 5,000lb, a power level which became standard for all production Nenes. This increased power provided for TS409 raised the maximum speed from 542 to 580mph. At 15,000ft the speed was raised from 552 to 568mph.

Following its initial flight trials at the A&AEE Boscombe Down, the prototype E.10/44 was displayed at the first postwar SBAC Display at Radlett in September 1946. It was the second prototype, TS413 completed to naval specification E.1/45 with folding wingtips, that acquired the type name Attacker F1. It was first flown on 17 June 1947 by Mike Lithgow and different from the first prototype in a number of details. The fin size was reduced, but the tailplane was increased in size; the flaps were modified and lift spoilers were fitted above the wing; balanced aileron tabs replaced spring tabs; the air intakes were modified; extra fuel tanks were fitted aft; the main undercarriage legs were modified to absorb the increased deck-landing loads and the pilot's safety was improved by the addition of a Martin-Baker ejection seat.

The directional 'snaking' experienced when flying the first prototype was even more apparent from the first flight of the second prototype, occurring at all speeds. The problem was corrected before the second flight by fitting beading from the top of the rudder, to the bottom of the tab. The aircraft safely achieved a speed of 375kts at 20,000ft, equivalent to Mach 0.823, and development then concentrated on the operation and effect on handling of the lift spoilers.

A series of some 30 airfield dummy deck landings (ADDLs) were flown in preparation for deck landing trials on HMS *Illustrious*, commencing on 28 October 1947. These trials were shared by Mike Lithgow, Lt-Cdr E. M. (Winkle) Brown of the RAE and Lt S. Orr of the A&AEE. Mike Lithgow's flight-test report considered that the average pilot should have no difficulty in landing the Attacker, providing the correct procedures were followed. The major problem encountered was the shearing of the arrester hook from the V-frame to which it was attached, during the preliminary trials, but this was corrected before the deck trials themselves. Further trouble was experienced with the hook arrangement during the trials causing a two-week break while further modifications were made. The tailwheel was considered unusual for a jet aircraft and, although it was not an outstanding aircraft, it performed reasonably well in service as the Navy's first operational jet fighter. Lt Orr found a tendency for the aircraft to float on approach, but the aerodynamic spoilers proved to be efficient enough.

A second series of sea trials were observed by officers of the US Navy, one of whom commented on the landing gear configuration. It was suggested that the tail-down approach gave a good aerodynamic braking effect. The tail down attitude was an advantage for the catapult launch where high wing incidence was required.

A proposal to use the prototype Attackers as engine test-beds was considered. In place of the 4,500lb-thrust Nene engine, the Attacker Mk 2 was proposed as TS409, powered by a 5,000lb-thrust de Havilland Ghost II as Specification 510. Further developments under Specification 527 suggested the fitting of the 6,000lb-thrust Rolls-Royce Avon or Tay engines. Other developments included the fitting of a 270gal ventral fuel tank on TS413, but this prototype crashed killing the A&AEE pilot, Lt T. J. A. King-Joyce RN, in June 1948.

With the loss of TS413, TS409 was brought up to Naval standard to undertake trials for the Attacker as a Royal Naval fighter. In September 1948, the Admiralty placed a production order for 60 Attacker Mk 1s, the plan being to deliver the complete batch by the end of March 1951. To facilitate early deliveries to allow the Fleet Air Arm to gain operational jet experience as soon as possible, the need was to produce a stock aircraft with the minimum of changes. TS409 commenced its naval development programme on 5 March 1949 and within six weeks had made 22 general handling flights, with particular attention to elevator and trim angles with various combinations of flap and spoiler settings.

Flight testing of the prototype continued in the evaluation of airbrake installation, the lack of which had been previously criticised, and to give naval pilots ADDL training in preparation for actual landings on HMS *Illustrious*. The airbrakes were found necessary due to lack of deceleration of the streamlined jet aircraft without the advantage of propeller braking on the approach to land.

Another problem encountered was the rudder locking over under certain sideslip conditions, particularly when the central fuel tank was fitted. It was thought

this may have been the cause of the loss of TS413 as well as production aircraft WA477, killing Supermarine test pilot Peter Robarts. The cure was found to be fitting of a dorsal fin which also improved directional control, and became a feature of the production aircraft.

The third prototype, TS416, joined the development programme with its maiden flight on 24 January 1950, and was the first to be fitted with a pressure cabin. This prototype featured a number of refinements as a result of earlier experience, examples being

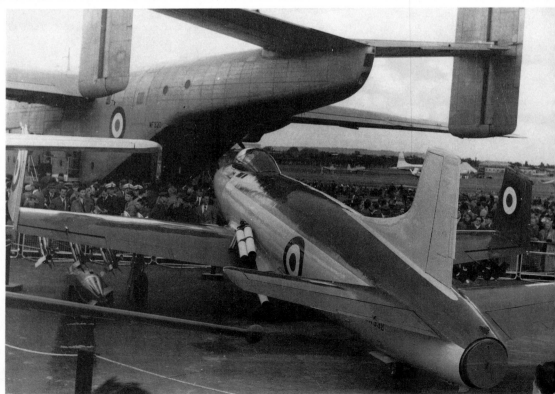

Above:
First production Attacker F1, WA469, without the additional dorsal fin, pictured during flight-testing at Chilbolton. *Vickers*

enlarged air intakes and the setting back of the wings around 13in. However, such was the rush to put the Attacker into service, the Mk 1s were completed to the earlier configuration.

It was also becoming apparent that the jet engine would allow aircraft to achieve much higher speeds than was possible with propeller aircraft. At the beginning of 1948, jets started breaking the various speed records, the Meteors achieving the absolute speed record, putting it out of reach of the Attacker. The Meteor also achieved 542mph in the 100km closed-circuit record, but when Mike Lithgow reached around 570mph in a practice, Supermarine was encouraged to try for the record. The selected course near the Supermarine test airfield at Chilbolton was officially surveyed at 100.136km, and on 26 February 1948 the record was raised to 564.881mph, despite poor visibility on the day of the attempt. Better visibility could have seen a better result, as was shown on a subse-

quent occasion when 570mph was again achieved, only 20mph below the top speed in level flight.

The next month Mike Lithgow flew the Attacker prototype to Paris at the invitation of the French Air Force and Navy. He had the unique opportunity to fly along the Champs-Elysees in Paris at as low an altitude as he wished, something that would never be allowed now. After flying over the Arc de Triomphe at 600mph, the return to Hurn near Bournemouth was made in under 25 minutes.

In July 1950 the prototype TS409 was flown by Mike Lithgow to Sherburn-in-Elmet to take part in the SBAC Challenge Cup at the National Air Races. The 570mph over the 100km course was achieved on this occasion, winning the trophy for Mike Lithgow. Even better speeds were anticipated at the same event at Hatfield in June 1951, but bad weather caused the event to be cancelled.

Various design exercises were looked at with the Attacker including a two-seat version, the fitting of floats similar to the Spitfire installation and jet deflection was considered as a means of reducing landing speed. RATOG tests were tried to reduce take-off run with eight rockets mounted in pairs above and below each wing.

Above left:
The third production Attacker F1, later to serve with 800 Squadron, was shown at the 1950 SBAC Farnborough Air Show. *M. J. F. Bowyer*

Left:
Attacker FB2, WK338, at the SBAC display at Farnborough in 1952 with rocket projectiles under the wings, and rocket-assisted take-off above and below the wing roots. *J. M. G. Gradidge*

The first Attacker, of a total of 181 to be built, WA469, was flown by Mike Lithgow on 5 April 1950, 18 months after the placing of the contract, to be followed soon after by R4000, the first for Pakistan, the sole export customer for the Attacker.

During a test flight on WA409, Les Colquhoun, one of the Supermarine test pilots, qualified for the award of the George Medal. The purpose of the flight on 23 May 1950 was to assess high Mach number behaviour and the effectiveness of the dive brakes. Two dives were made up to 400kts with the dive brakes being operated. In a further dive over the Supermarine production airfield at South Marston, near Swindon to 430kts, when the airbrakes were opened there was a sudden nose-up trim change, followed by a sharp nose-down trim change. During the nose-up trim change there was a loud bang and the starboard wingtip folded up into the vertical position. The aircraft momentarily dropped its starboard wing, but with application of full port rudder it was possible to fly more or less straight and level. With speed reduced to 270kts, it was decided to attempt a landing. With undercarriage down, a wide lefthand circuit was flown using the rudder, since the folded wingtip locked the ailerons solid. On the final approach, flaps were lowered and the speed was reduced to 210kts, but control became difficult as the speed decayed. The airfield boundary was crossed at 200kts, followed by a landing, the aircraft using all but 10yds of available runway. The port tyre burst in the last 100yds, causing the aircraft to swing to the left, but no further damage was sustained.

Deck landing proving trials continued using TS413, and modifications embodied retrospectively on all aircraft included the new dorsal fin, flat sided elevators and lighter aileron controls. Structured provision for a bomb-carrying beam had already been built into the design, making it relatively simple to comply with a Navy fighter-bomber requirement by adding the necessary electrical wiring. The 55th production Attacker, WA529, first flew on 7 January 1952 as the first of six FB1s.

The fighter-bomber role was further developed in the FB2 which was powered by a Rolls-Royce Nene 7 engine, later designated Nene 102, improvements including an electric starter, a metal-framed cockpit canopy, provision for six rockets in two tiers under each wing and other refinements. The first Attacker FB2, WK319, flew on 25 April 1952, a total of 84 being produced for the Fleet Air Arm.

Below:
The export version of the Attacker, G-15-110, was shown at Farnborough in 1951, fitted with the ventral fuel tank and a range of warloads. *J. D. R. Rawlings*

3
Attacker in Service

When the Attacker entered service with 800 Squadron at RNAS Ford on 22 August 1951 it became the premier jet squadron of the Fleet Air Arm, the aircraft being the first jet fighter in frontline service with the Royal Navy. The aircraft were equipped with Martin-Baker ejection seats, provisions for Rocket Assisted Take-off Gear (RATOG) and a bulbous ventral 250gal drop tank to increase the endurance of the thirsty early jet engines. No 800 Squadron was equipped with a total of eight Attacker F1s, the commanding officer being Lt-Cdr George Baldwin, later an outspoken supporter of the fixed wing Fleet Air Arm. On 4 March 1952 the squadron embarked on HMS *Eagle* for a three-week training period, and then alternated between Ford and HMS *Eagle*, apart from a brief period at Hal Far in Malta in April 1954. In December 1952 the squadron strength was increased to 12 F1s when they received some of the complement of the

short-lived 890 Squadron. HMS *Eagle* had been serving both in home waters and the Mediterranean, but 800 Squadron finally disbanded at Ford on 1 June 1954, later reforming at Brawdy with Sea Hawks.

Above:
No 800 Squadron, FAA, Attacker F1, WA492, visiting South Marston a couple of months after the squadron was formed at RNAS Ford. *F. G. Swanborough*

Right:
No 800 Squadron Attacker FB2, WK341, used RNAS Ford as its shore base, and went to sea on HMS Eagle. *J. D. R. Rawlings*

27

Above:
No 800 Squadron, FAAs, Attackers are seen aboard HMS *Eagle* as she passes Southsea. *FAA Museum*

Left:
Attacker F1 WA496; 101/J of 800 Squadron aboard HMS *Eagle*. *FAA Museum*

Below:
Attacker FB2 WK322; 102/J of 800 Squadron in barrier engagement on HMS *Eagle*, 4 March 1953. *FAA Museum*

The second Attacker squadron was 803 at Ford on 26 November 1951 led by Lt-Cdr T. D. Handley, also to serve a rotation between Ford and HMS *Eagle* similar to 800 Squadron. Like 800 Squadron, 803 also received four Attacker F1s when 890 Squadron disbanded. When 800 Squadron disbanded, 803 went on to serve abroad the RN carriers *Albion* and *Centaur* before its disbandment on 4 November 1955.

As already mentioned 890 Squadron operated Attackers, reforming at Ford on 30 January 1952, but it was not until 22 April that it was commissioned under the command of Lt-Cdr R. W. Kearsley who remained in charge until disbandment on 3 December 1952. The reason for its short service was that the main duty was to act as a pool to provide aircraft and pilots to the other two squadrons. In October 1952 the unit embarked on HMS *Eagle* where it disbanded two months later.

Top:

No 803 Squadron FAA Attacker FB2, WP292, also operated off HMS *Eagle* when not shore-based at RNAS Ford. *J. D. R. Rawlings*

Above:

No 890 Squadron, FAA, Attacker FB2s at RNAS Ford in 1952. *FAA Museum*

Before the Attacker passed from frontline service it was able to participate in Her Majesty the Queen's Review of the Royal Navy at Spithead in 1953.

A number of secondline units also operated Attackers. The first was 787 Squadron, a trials unit formed at West Raynham in January 1951. The initial commander was Lt-Cdr B. H. C. Nation, followed by Lt-Cdr Campbell, and later Lt-Cdr S. G. Orr who had participated in the service trials of the aircraft. There was a detachment to St Davids in mid-1952 and the squadron operated all versions of the Attacker before disbanding on 16 January 1956.

No 703 Squadron formed with Attacker F1s at Ford in July and August alongside 800 Squadron, acting as trials unit. It was aircraft of 703 composite unit, which did the initial carrier trials on the new HMS *Eagle*. By May 1953 the unit's duties included the testing and calibration of catapult and arrester gears after carrier refits, as well as testing equipment developed by the Safety Equipment School and Medical Air School, both at Gosport. All versions of the Attacker

served with 703 Squadron until the final aircraft left in August 1955.

No 702 Squadron received Attacker F1s at Culdrose in March 1952 to undertake the conversion of piston engine-trained pilots on to jet fighters. However, on 26 August 1952 the unit was renumbered 738 Squadron under a reorganisation of FAA training units, and returned to Sea Fury training at the shore base of Lossiemouth.

The major Attacker training unit was 736 Squadron, reformed at Culdrose on 26 August 1952, replacing 702 Squadron. It was known as an Advanced Jet Flying School and the commanding offi-

cer was Lt-Cdr N. Perrett who transferred from 702 Squadron. In addition to the single-seat Attackers, as no two-seat training variant existed, Meteor T7s were used for conversion training for jet techniques, particularly the lower acceleration on take-off and the reduced drag on landing. As part of the Naval Air Fighter School, the unit moved to Lossiemouth in November 1953, where weather conditions were more suitable for flying training. Attacker F1s and FB2s were used by 736 Squadron until replaced in August 1954 by Sea Hawks, the Meteors being replaced by Vampire T22s.

No 767 Squadron moved to RNAS Stretton on 20 September 1952, where it received Attackers in February 1953. The duty of the squadron was to provide training for deck landing control officers, flying continual circuits and landings. With the introduction of the Mirror Landing Aid, 767 became the Signal Officers Training Squadron, but soon after the Attackers departed.

Below:
Attacker FB2, WP282 of 787 Squadron – a trials unit based at West Raynham – with underwing carriers for practice bombs. *M. P. Marsh*

Above:
Attacker FB2 WZ277 with 703 Squadron, FAA.
FAA Museum

No 700 Squadron reformed at RNAS Ford on 18 August 1955 as the Trials and Requirements Unit, replacing 703 and 771 Squadrons. Attacker FB2s served from August 1955 until February 1956 as part of a wide collection of aircraft in current FAA service.

With the re-equipment of the frontline FAA squadrons with Sea Hawks, a number of Attackers were surplus and put into store. However, the re-equipping of the RNVR squadrons gave a new lease of life to these relatively short-lifespan aircraft. No 718 Squadron was reformed at RNAS Stretton on 25 April 1955 to convert the RNVR pilots of 1831 Squadron from propeller aircraft. Aircraft used were Attacker FB2s with Vampire T22s being used for dual conversion, and the commanding officer was Lt-Cdr W. C. Cook. The squadron moved to Honiley in July 1955 to train the pilots of 1833 Squadron, disbanding on 31 December 1955 when its task was complete.

As already mentioned, the RNVR units were allocated Attackers, 1831 Squadron at Stretton with seven FB2s and Vampire T22s in May 1955. The unit was part of the Northern Air Division, having previously operated Sea Furies, but disbandment came for all the RNVR Squadrons on 10 March 1957 in the defence cuts.

No 1832 Squadron received their first jet equipment at RAF Benson in July 1955 with the first two Vampire T22s followed the next month by the first of eight Attacker FB2s. By November the Attackers had moved on and were replaced by Sea Hawks the next January, disbanding coming in March 1957. The Attackers used RAF Benson due to the unsuitability of nearby RNAS Culham for jet fighter operations. In effect the aircraft were operated on a pooled basis with

1835 and 1836 Squadrons who were all part of the Southern Air Division.

The final RNVR unit equipped with Attackers was 1833 Squadron, based at Bramcote as part of the Midland Air Division. Seven Attacker FB2s arrived in October 1955, necessitating a move to RAF Honiley where hard runways were available. When 1833 Squadron was disbanded in March 1957, it was the last flying unit at Honiley before closure.

Following the disbandment of the RNVR Squadrons the majority of the Attackers left in flying condition were ferried to RNAS Abbotsinch, now Glasgow International Airport. About 70 aircraft were received and scrapping continued with completion by mid-1958. However, one aircraft survived, WA437 as a gate guardian at the airfield, eventually finding its way to the Fleet Air Arm Museum at Yeovilton.

Support units allocated some of the surplus Attackers were the Fleet Requirements Unit (FRU) at Hurn, which opened on 1 September 1952 and used Attackers from October 1955 until February 1957, and Airwork which formed at Brawdy on 5 January 1950 and operated Attackers at St Davids from December 1955 to January 1957.

Top right:
No 1832 (RNVR) Squadron operated Attacker FB2, WP289, at RAF Benson from August 1955.
J. D. R. Rawlings

Centre right:
No 1832 (RNVR) Squadron was part of the Southern Air Division operating Attacker FB2s, including WZ273, from RAF Benson. *J. D. R. Rawlings*

Bottom right:
Attacker FB2, WK320, of 1833 (RNVR) Squadron which formed part of the Midland Air Division at Honiley. *M. P. Marsh*

Top:
Following the disbandment of the RNVR units in March 1957, their aircraft, including the Attacker FB2 WP302 of 1833 Squadron, were stored at RNAS Abbotsinch pending their ultimate fate as scrap. *M. J. F. Bowyer*

Above:
Attacker FB1, WA531, which served with the Airwork FRU at Brawdy and St Davids, joined many other Attackers in storage at Abbotsinch in 1958 before being scrapped. *M. J. F. Bowyer*

Above:
Attacker FB1, WA533, seen here been broken up at Bramcote in mid-1957, had served with 736 Squadron FAA, the advanced jet flying school at Lossiemouth.
Woodward

Below:
The first of six Attacker FB1s, WA529 was used for fire practice at RNAS Ford in June 1958.
J. M. G. Gradidge

Above:

The only export sale of the Attacker was to Pakistan, R4031 passed through Luqa, Malta, on delivery in January 1953. *R. C. B. Ashworth*

In the early part of 1950 it was decided to send an Attacker on a demonstration tour of the Middle East, accompanied by a Vickers Valetta as a support aircraft. The air forces in question mostly operated obsolete propeller-driven aircraft, but the jet aircraft was limited in its appeal due to the high first cost, and subsequent running costs.

A customs departure was made from Manston on 19 May, the plan being to use as many as possible of the regular RAF facilities en-route. Nice was the first stop and then the route went via North Africa to Tunis where the first impromptu demo was held. The next destination was Cairo via Tripoli and El Adem, the Egyptian Air Force being considered a possible customer. Beirut was the next port of call, reached by flying at a safe distance off the Israeli coast, but at that time there were no jets or missiles to catch the unwary, especially at a cruising speed of Mach 0.8.

The tour then continued to Damascus and Baghdad where rising sand over the featureless desert was a major hazard. Tehran was the most easterly point on the tour where demonstrations were made to the Shah of Iran, who was almost tempted to fly the aircraft himself.

On the return to Baghdad, one of the fuel tanks sprung a leak and had to be sealed off on landing, reducing the range of the aircraft. Following another transit at Damascus, Ankara was reached for demos to the Turkish Air Force, followed later by a visit to Athens to show the aircraft to the Greeks. A new fuel tank was fitted in Athens, and the return continued via Rome where a short demo was flown in support of the Valetta. During the entire six-week tour, over 7,000 nautical miles were flown and the only snags were one hydraulic pump failure and the leaking fuel tank. Not even a tyre was changed. Regrettably, no sales resulted from this tour.

One export success was in 1949 when 36 Attackers were ordered by the Royal Pakistan Air Force as its initial jet equipment in the early build up of the air force. All the jet aircraft were delivered from South Marston mainly by Supermarine pilots. During these delivery flights, the aircraft operated in pairs for safety as they over flew 85,348 miles of sea and 54,568 miles of desert. The route chosen was to allow stage lengths of about 500 nautical miles, equivalent to about half the still air range at best cruising height and with ventral drop tank. Also, the prevailing weather conditions and nature of the terrain dictated a more southerly route, although a stop at Cyprus was preferred to Cairo. The average time for a delivery flight was one week, although it was achieved inside three days by three pairs of aircraft. In service with Pakistan, the Attackers were used as fighter-bombers, being capable of carrying up to two 1,000lb bombs and eight rocket-propelled projectiles under the wings.

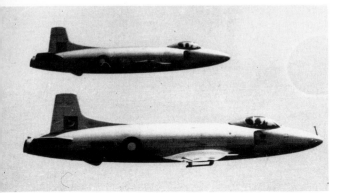

Left:

Royal Pakistan Air Force Attackers. *RAF Museum*

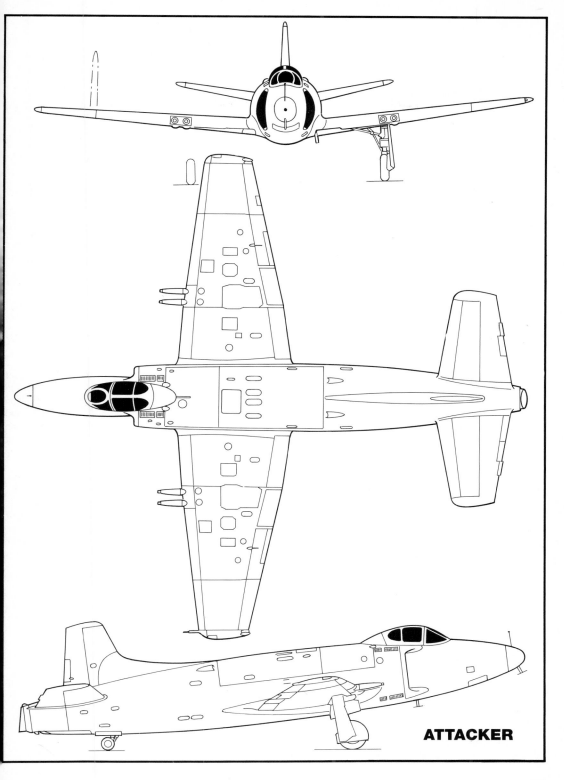

ATTACKER

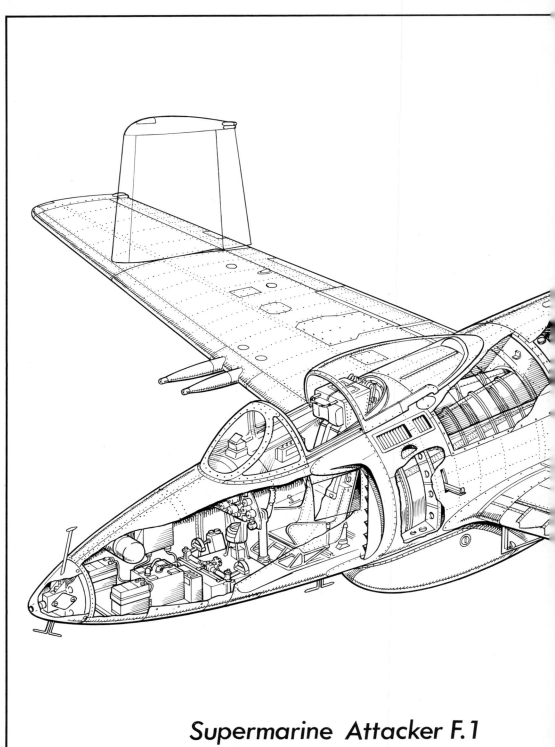

Supermarine Attacker F.1

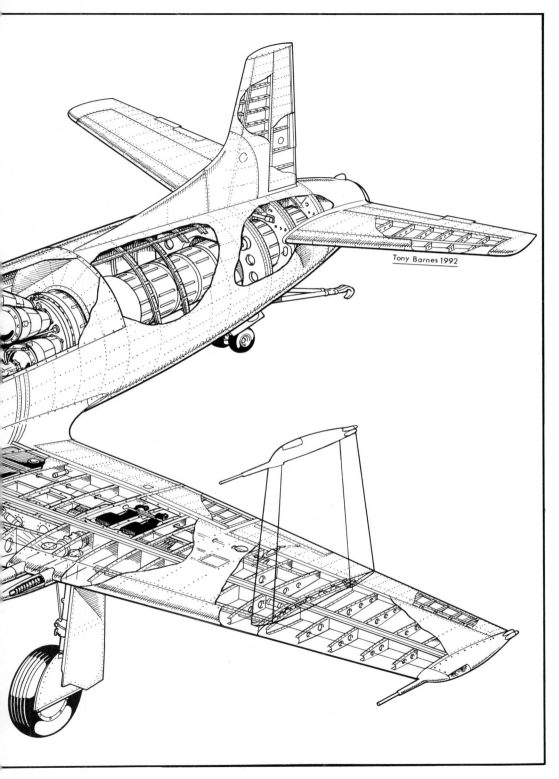

Tony Barnes 1992

39

4
Swept Wing Development — The Type 510 to the 545

From the results of German research during World War 2 it was realised that by sweeping back the wings and tail surfaces of jet-powered aircraft, drag rise at high subsonic speeds was delayed, allowing still greater speeds. While this was realised quite quickly in the USA, where the North American F-86 Sabre was produced – and also in the USSR with the MiG-15 – Britain took a little longer to take advantage of this major improvement. The irony of the MiG-15

Below:
The Supermarine 510/517, VV106, became 7175M in January 1955 when it was grounded for technical training at Melksham and Halton. It was preserved for a while at Cardington and is now part of the RAF Museum collection at Cosford. *J. M. G. Gradidge*

in particular was that it was powered by a Russian equivalent of the Rolls-Royce Nene engine donated by the British Government as a goodwill gesture after the end of World War 2.

Eventually the British Government went for a low cost development programme, covering the adaptation of the two current straight wing jet fighters to the swept wing configurations: the Hawker P1040 was one example and the Attacker the other. Supermarine took a basic Attacker fuselage and fitted 40° swept back wings and tail-surfaces, to Specification E.41/46. The Supermarine aircraft was designated the Type 510, the purpose of the aircraft being to investigate the flight characteristics of swept wings at high subsonic speed, with a maximum speed of 610kts.

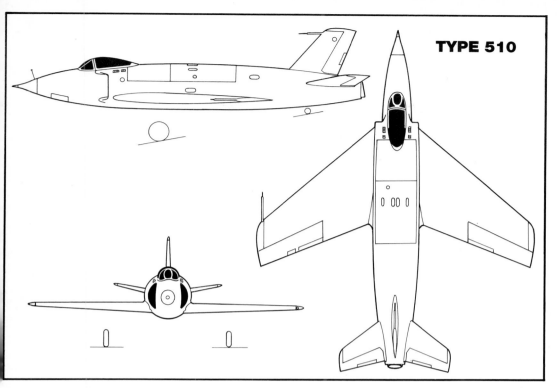

TYPE 510

The contract covered the construction of the two prototypes, VV106 and VV119, both built at Hursley Park and each powered by a single Rolls-Royce Nene 2 engine. The basic Attacker fuselage was adapted to accept the new flying surfaces, which in the case of the wings had to be mounted further forward to maintain an acceptable centre of gravity. The original tailwheel undercarriage was retained, but no naval features were included initially.

The first prototype, VV106, was moved by road to Boscombe Down and, after reassembly, Mike Lithgow made the maiden flight on 28 December 1948, 21 months after the development contract was placed.

It was immediately obvious that the high-speed characteristics of the new layout were exceptional and in a matter of only a few weeks Mach numbers close to 0.90 were being achieved. Thoughts turned to changing this modest experimental aircraft into a fighter. The American equivalent was the North American F-86, as already mentioned, upon which the US Government had invested large sums of money. In contrast Supermarine had to modify the second prototype with a nosewheel undercarriage and gun installation at their own expense due to lack of funding. The

Right:
Supermarine 510, VV106, makes a high-speed flypast at Farnborough in September 1949. *Vickers*

official policy of not investing in high speed aircraft research between 1946 and 1950 took a great deal of effort and expense from which to recover.

Despite the good high speed performance of the Type 510, there were handling problems at both low and high speeds which made it unsuitable as such for squadron service. Tip stalling of the wing was experienced at low speed, causing pitch up. Provision had been made for leading-edge slats on the outboard section of the wing, but they were found unnecessary and remained locked up. In July 1949 they were removed.

At high speeds, a very strong lateral trim change required full right control column movement to keep the wings level. This was effective until Mach 0.93 when control was lost altogether, limiting Mach to this level. To try and improve controllability a servodyne provided power assistance to the ailerons, but it was obvious that for higher speeds, not only would there have to be some aerodynamic improvements, but also the full provision of power control.

The Rolls-Royce Nene 2 engine which developed a static thrust of 5,000lb was also not trouble free, one engine failure causing a forced landing at Boscombe Down on 17 March 1949. There was severe engine vibration when power was reduced below 6,000rpm. When taken down to 4,000rpm directional stability was affected, the aircraft yawing left and right approximately 5° in a series of random darts. The cause was found to be a function of both airspeed and engine speed, and was found to originate from turbulent airflow in the engine air intakes. The cure was to raise and redesign the boundary layer bleeds above and below the intake lip and to fit a more robust Attacker-type front engine mount.

At an engine speed of 12,300rpm a speed of 630 to 635mph was reached at 10,000 to 15,000ft. The early flights were with a rounded nose cone, but speed increased slightly when a pointed one was fitted. Another fault found during early trials was the loss of the cockpit hood in flight, after which the hood jettison mechanism was modified.

The Supermarine 510 made its public debut at the SBAC Display at Farnborough in September 1949 during which the aircraft made six daily demonstrations. Later the same month the aircraft went to Boscombe Down for initial service evaluation where it was generally well received. The lift was considerably improved at high speeds due to better high Mach number drag, despite limitations to the maximum usable lift-coefficient in the transonic region. The sweepback did, however, introduce longitudinal instability leading up to the stall, particularly at high altitude. At 40,000ft the aircraft was practically confined to straight flight due to limited manoeuvrability. The aircraft did not suffer from the predicted problems of high wing sweepback, and was easy and pleasant to fly. It had no tendency to snake or dutch-roll, and the ailerons gave a high rate of roll at low altitudes. The tailwheel undercarriage was criticised, the recommendation being that with a tricycle undercarriage and improved elevator control, it formed the basis of a good fighter.

In July 1950 the Type 510 went to the RAE at Farnborough where, although the aircraft was found to have a generally poor finish, it was appreciated that it was only a quick conversion to assess the viability of swept wings and tail surfaces. Comparative tests were made between the Type 510, by this time known as the Swift, and the F-86 Sabre. As would be expected, the Sabre proved to be overall superior in performance, but at 25,000ft they were about equal in terms of speed. The Sabre obviously gained due to better production finish and the greater thrust of the engine.

Following these trials the Type 510 returned to Supermarine to be modified for naval testing, as a possible follow-on for the Attacker. An A-type arrester hook was fitted under the fuselage and the normal 13.5ft/sec main undercarriage oleos were replaced by 16ft/sec units to absorb the high landing rates on deck operations. The all-up weight was increased to 12,700lb, additional take-off boost being provided by the provision of four RATO units grouped above and below the wing root trailing edges.

Mike Lithgow recommended the flight trials in this configuration on 14 September 1950 and it was then delivered to Farnborough for dummy deck landings in preparation for the first deck landing by a swept wing jet on 8 November by Lt Jock Elliot on HMS *Illustrious*. A total of 12 landings and rocket assisted take-offs were achieved in one day, three by Lt Elliot, and the remainder shared by Mike Lithgow and Lt-Cdr D. G. Parker of Boscombe Down, later to reach the rank of Rear Admiral. Generally, there was a 50kt wind speed along the deck, the carrier travelling at up to 25kts, and the sea state was fairly stable for all landings. Take-off with only two rockets fired resulted in an acceptable run of 500ft, with a slight starboard wing drop.

Approach speeds were in the region of 124 to 134kts indicated, resulting in good landings with excellent oleo rebound characteristics. Deck landing proved straightforward with refuelling, rocket change and other turn round activities allowing landings to be made on average every 20min.

The next day the trials continued with three further landings, but a fuel pressure warning light required a return to the shore base. On this latter take-off, the rockets failed to produce full thrust on one side causing an alarming swing to the left. As a result the wingtip hit the top of a gun turret, but Lt-Cdr Parker retained control and safely flew the aircraft to its home base.

Following repairs, the aircraft returned to the RAE for more development flying before removal of the naval equipment. It then was flown at Farnborough on high Mach number trials during 1951 and 1952, but on

Top:
Supermarine 510, VV106, makes the first landing by a swept-wing jet aircraft on a carrier, HMS *Illustrious*, 17 November 1950. *RAF Museum*

Above:
Supermarine 510, VV106, aboard HMS *Illustrious* for deck trials on 17 November 1950. *FAA Museum*

14 December 1952 a wheels-up landing was made due to failure of the main undercarriage to come down.

During this programme of high speed research it became obvious that modifications would have to be made to improve controllability at high speeds. The elevator spring tab was removed to reduce a possible flutter source and a full power control was provided with an elevator of reduced chord. However, a more practical solution was to hinge the whole rear fuselage and jet pipe just aft of the fin to give up to 4° of movement, while keeping the tailplane fixed. Work on this started at Supermarine on 10 July 1953 and because of this relatively major change the new Type No 517 was allocated. This somewhat radical solution worked, but was initially too fast acting, and worked well when the gearing was reduced.

Following its wheels-up landing, the aircraft was repaired and flown again by Dave Morgan, Supermarine test pilot, on 2 September 1953, and the aircraft continued its contribution to high subsonic speed research until 14 January 1955 when it was allocated to RAF Melksham as a ground instructional airframe. It soon moved to RAF Halton, and when it had ceased to be of use to the trainee engineers there, it was saved from destruction and put on open display at RAF Cardington, in company with its contemporary, the Hawker P1052. The Type 517 then moved to the RAF Colerne Museum but upon the closure of that fine collection, this swept wing research aircraft joined the RAF Cosford Museum.

The second prototype Swift, VV119, was externally similar to the first prototype, but due to internal changes it was designated the Type 528. The aircraft was built to the same specification, but one of the major changes was provision for afterburning the Nene engine to increase the power.

Meanwhile the design office had been busy looking at operational versions of the Swift, the Type 520 having four wing-mounted 20mm cannon, and an export version proposed for Australia had a longer pointed nose and a more powerful Nene or Tay engine. A nosewheel undercarriage was being seen as desirable, although official policy did not recognise this need.

The prototype 528, VV119, was first flown by Mike Lithgow on 27 March 1950. The fuel capacity was increased to 600gal, the hope being that there would be sufficient endurance to attempt the four runs at reheat power on the absolute speed record. However, the need to consider the aircraft as a possible fighter gained priority over the thought of a speed record attempt and the aircraft went back to the drawing board on 6 May for major modifications.

The most obvious external change was to extend the nose and fit a nosewheel undercarriage. Other major changes included enlarging the rear fuselage to accommodate the reheat; a new tail cone to increase the taper of the fuselage to the smaller jet pipe diam-

eter; larger reshaped air intakes; provision for wing-mounted guns; stronger steel-framed cockpit canopy; and an improved fuel system. The wing area at the centre section was increased by reducing the sweep-back at the trailing edge root end. These drastic modifications to the prototype increased its length by 4ft and the original tailwheel was retained in the event of a tail-down landing.

With the new designation Type 535, the aircraft flew again from Boscombe Down on 23 August 1950, the first use of reheat being a week later. This was the only reheat application for the Nene engine, but the earlier elevator buffet was eliminated by the change in shape of the fuselage. The aircraft appeared at the SBAC display at Farnborough during September of 1950, making its public debut.

Aerodynamic testing of the prototype continued through the remainder of 1950 and into 1951, leading to measured speed checks of the aircraft in July. Level flight speeds at various altitudes were recorded as 622mph at 15,000ft, 609mph at 26,000ft and 583mph at 35,000ft. In October 1951, Sqn Ldr Dave Morgan took over the testing of VV119, having recently joined the Supermarine team. The aircraft was used in the research for pilots' anti-gravity clothing from 30,000ft, and it became a star under the name of 'Prometheus' in the film *Sound Barrier*, much of which was made at the de Havilland airfield at Hatfield and at Chilbolton.

On January 1952 the aircraft was slightly damaged on landing, but was flying again by mid-March. Airbrakes were tried on the upper surfaces of the wings, but caused considerable buffet at high speeds, while the existing flaps provided sufficient aerodynamic braking. Selection was by a two-position switch, which rapidly selected 35° or 55°, allowing a reduction from top speed to 160kts at low altitude in less than one minute. The aircraft could also descend from 40,000ft at a rate of 25,000ft/min without exceeding Mach 0.79.

The wing-drop experienced on VV106 at high speed was still apparent to a lesser extent on VV119, but the power assisted manual controls had a limited

Top right:
Vickers Supermarine E.41/46 Type 535 prototype, VV119, after conversion to a nosewheel undercarriage and powered by a Rolls-Royce Nene 3 engine. *MOS*

Centre right:
Supermarine Type 535, VV119, makes a flypast at the manufacturer's test airfield at Chilbolton. *Vickers*

Bottom right:
The Supermarine Type 535, VV119, was demonstrated at Farnborough in September 1951. *J. D. R. Rawlings*

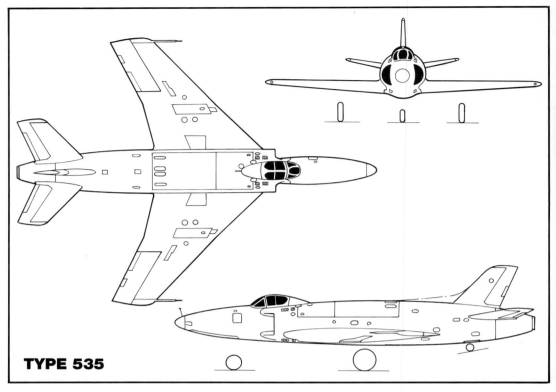

TYPE 535

effect at high transonic speeds. Missile trials were carried out in 1955 by fitting dummy Fairey Fireflash missiles under the wings to investigate the effects on drag and handling. Two dummy weapons were carried up to Mach 0.95 and four up to Mach 0.90. There was little change in overall handling apart from an increase in roll inertia.

The flight-testing duties of the aircraft ceased on 28 September 1955, when it was allocated to RAF Halton for ground instruction with the identity 7285M. Unlike VV106, the Type 535 was scrapped at Halton at the end of its useful life.

The Supermarine Type 541 looked very similar to the Type 535, but was the next step towards a production standard Swift fighter. The major improvement in this fighter prototype, WJ960, was the fitting of an axial flow Rolls-Royce Avon RA7 engine developing 7,500lbs of thrust, in place of the earlier Nene. To conserve fuel and maintain a reasonable endurance no reheat was fitted to this engine, its power being 50% better than the earlier aircraft.

This interim fighter prototype first flew on 1 August 1951, and the benefit of increased power was immediately shown with the improved take-off and climb performance. However, due to aerodynamic limitations already experienced with the earlier prototypes, the aircraft was not capable of supersonic speeds. The external changes included improved air

intake, larger span ailerons, a small dorsal fillet to the fin, modified tail-cone and flared out wingtips. The retractable tailwheel was retained, but with doors, and a variable incidence tailplane was fitted giving travel from -9 to +4°.

Preparations were in hand for the public demonstrations at the SBAC display at Farnborough, but the new Avon engine was not entirely reliable. On 3 August Mike Lithgow was flying in formation with a Spitfire for publicity photos of the old and the new. However when power was increased on completion of the exercise, a massive uncontrollable vibration occurred, followed by the engine failing. The vibration continued until speed reduced by the use of the very effective airbrakes, and it was possible to glide the ten miles to Chilbolton for a safe landing. The vibration was found to be caused by aileron flutter, which was soon corrected allowing Dave Morgan to continue the flying programme.

Unfortunately, on 8 September, two days before the aircraft was due to appear in the Farnborough show, Dave Morgan was on the final approach to land, when at 800ft the engine stopped without warning. Between the aircraft and the runway was the River Test in a steep-sided valley 400ft from the threshold. The only alternative was to select the undercarriage up and turn downwind to a slightly less rough force landing area. After skidding under high tension telegraph

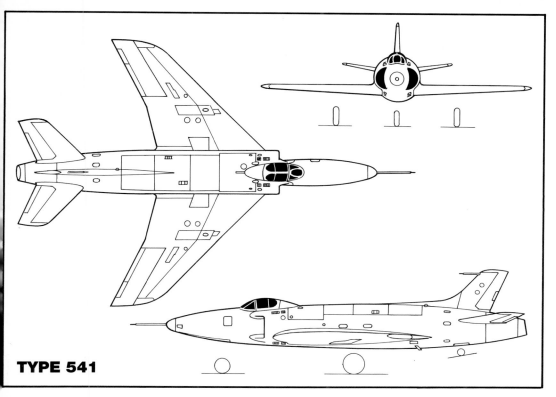

TYPE 541

lines, the aircraft hit an apple tree with the starboard wing and a brick-built privy – fortunately unoccupied – with the other wing.

Despite this rough treatment, the aircraft proved its toughness; it was repaired and flying again within three months. It suffered a further engine failure on 8 April 1952, but the problem was cured by 11 July, when Dave Morgan flew the aircraft to the Brussels Exhibition. It was therefore decided to attempt the London to Brussels record, and by flying at 12,000ft at a reduced throttle setting to conserve fuel, an average speed of 665.9mph was achieved over the 200.38 miles in a time of 18min/3.3sec. It was returned to Supermarine from Boscombe Down on 14 August 1953 for the installation of the variable incidence

Below:
The Rolls-Royce Avon-powered Supermarine Type 541, WJ960, pictured at Chilbolton, the experimental flight-test centre. *MOS*

Top:
The second type 541 prototype, WJ965, which was very similar to the production Swift Mk 1. *Vickers*

Above:
The Type 541 production prototype Swift, WJ965, which first flew on 18 July 1952, is shown here at Farnborough in September of the same year.
J. D. R. Rawlings

tailplane and geared aileron tabs, flying again in February 1954. In 1955 trials were made with nose-wheel braking and in 1956 the aircraft was moved to RAE Bedford for arrester barrier trials. Following a further accident, the aircraft was withdrawn from use on 15 September 1959 and sold for scrap.

The next prototype, WJ965, was much more representative of the production Swift, which made its maiden flight from Boscombe Down in the hands of Dave Morgan on 18 July 1952. The major differences were a shorter nose and improved cockpit to give the pilot a better view, modified air intakes for a more efficient engine, a new fin and repositioned wing. Fuel capacity was increased significantly and provision made for operational equipment.

During the early flight testing, wing and aileron flutter was experienced which was worse than before due to the weight saving reduction in wing skins. The cure was found to be full power-operated ailerons which at long last allowed the aircraft to be flown supersonically in a dive without loss of control. This was achieved for the first time on 26 February 1953.

Although very different, the ultimate single-engined jet fighter development used much of the experience gained with the Swift programme. This was the Type 545 designed to specification F/105D2 in competition with Hawker P.1083, the contract being placed in February 1952. This more advanced design with its area ruled fuselage and compound sweep-back on the wing leading edge promised a high performance, the Supermarine project clearly outclassing the Hawker aircraft which was cancelled in July 1953. Two prototypes of the Type 545 were ordered with the first one, XA181, planned to fly in the spring of 1954 followed by the second aircraft, XA186, in early 1955.

The aircraft was intended as a supersonic replacement for the Swift, and the crescent-shaped wing was sharply swept back 50° on the thicker inboard section, which housed the main undercarriage, and thinner with 30° sweep-back outer section for good high altitude performance. Although the swept tail surfaces were along similar lines to the Swift, another major difference was the moving forward of the engine air intakes to the nose, the orifice split by a centre-body avoiding the need for bypass bleed.

The engine initially selected was the 9,500lb thrust Rolls-Royce RA14 Avon, which could achieve

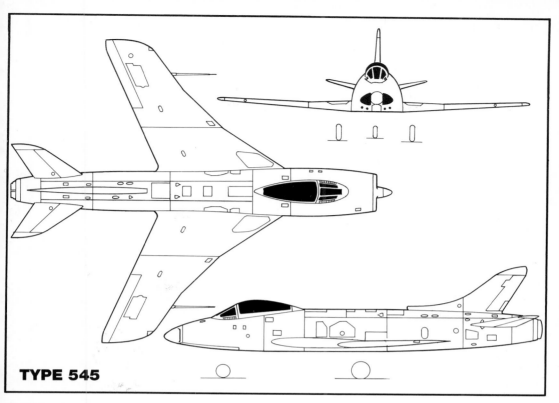

TYPE 545

14,500lb thrust with reheat. This should have given the aircraft a speed of Mach 1.3 in level flight, but as the delayed design programme progressed, it was realised that due to higher drag estimates, this performance would only be achieved in a dive. A development was offered using either the Rolls-Royce Avon RA35R or the RB106 to power the second prototype, which was expected to provide sufficient power to achieve Mach 1.68.

Around the latter part of 1954 the competing English Electric P1 was proving its much higher performance and capability, resulting in the cancelling of the second prototype 545 on 9 November, and the scrapping of the work in progress. Construction of the more complete first prototype continued, but as RAF interest waned in anticipation of the eventual entry into service of the Mach 2 Lightning, work was covered by the research specification E7/54. The intention was to deliver the aircraft to Farnborough for experimental flying following the initial manufacturer's trials. All provision for armament was removed and, powered by the RA28R Avon, the planned first flight

was to be in mid-1955. However, the remainder of the programme was cancelled in early 1955 when prototype 545, XA181, was structurally complete, and all work on developed versions ceased. The partially completed aircraft was moved to the College of Aeronautics at Cranfield for instructional purposes until it was scrapped in the early 1960s. The scrapping of this aircraft was unusual since the majority of the other historic aircraft used by Cranfield for instructional purposes found their way into museums, assuring their preservation.

Right:
The Supermarine 545 prototype, XA181, was never completed, and was preserved for a while for technical training at the College of Aeronautics at Cranfield. *J. M. G. Gradidge*

49

5

RAF Service With the Swift

In November 1950 an order was placed by the RAF for 100 production Swift day fighters, in addition to the two pre-production prototypes. All were to be powered by a single Rolls-Royce Avon axial flow jet engine developing 7,500lb thrust.

Of the development and trials batch of an initial 20 aircraft, the first two, WK194 and WK195, were built in the experimental department at Hursley Park. Subsequent production was set up at the South Marston factory. The Swift was reputedly the favoured aircraft over the rival Hawker Hunter, partly because of the better endurance of the Swift, made possible by the additional room for fuel in the bulbous fuselage developed around the larger diameter Nene engine.

The first production aircraft WK194, an F1, first flew on 25 August 1952 and was allocated to service trials at Boscombe Down, research flying at Farnborough and company development. When its flying duties were completed it became an instructional airframe at Kirkham in March 1956, being scrapped only six months later at No 33 MU Lyneham. The second production aircraft from the experimental department shared service trials at Boscombe with WK194. It became the F3 prototype and finally was used by Rolls-Royce for Avon reheat development.

The first Swift off the South Marston production line, WK196, first flew in March 1953 fitted with full-boosted flying controls. The Swift F1 was only armed with two 30mm Aden cannon underneath the cockpit,

but when it was decided to double this armament, the F1s were too far advanced to be modified.

The Swift F2 therefore featured four 30mm Aden cannon in the lower fuselage, with ammunition stored in a forward extension of the inboard section of the wing root leading edge. Production commenced with WK214, and finished with WK246, a total of 16 being completed. Many of these were not issued for operational service. However, the modified wing root resulted in a violent and uncontrollable pitch-up when g was applied at Mach 0.85 and above, a highly undesirable characteristic in a combat aircraft. When the pilot pulled back on the stick, the nose reared up and the aircraft flicked over on its back. This may be a useful manoeuvre in defence, but it would certainly not help in an attacking situation. The time taken for recovery also made the aircraft very vulnerable in combat.

In an attempt to overcome the problem a wing fence was fitted on the top surface of the wing and the leading edge was extended forward in a small step at about half-span. This did not prove to be a fully effective answer, the ideal cure being to move the centre of

Below:
The first production Swift F1, WK194, flew on 25 August 1952 and was used for development and trials at Chilbolton, Boscombe Down and Farnborough. *J. M. G. Gradidge*

Above:
The second production Swift F1, WK195, was used for Rolls-Royce Avon reheat development and became the F3 prototype. *J. M. G. Gradidge*

gravity forward. However, this could only be achieved by fixing heavy ballast weights in the nose, which limited the high altitude performance.

Despite these major problems, the Swift became the first swept-wing jet fighter to enter service with the RAF. No 56 Squadron at RAF Waterbeach in Cambridgeshire received its first F1 WK209 on 20 February 1954, followed by the first F2 on 30 August. A total of eight F1s had been delivered by

Right:
A rare photograph of six No 56 Squadron, RAF Swift F1s in formation, the lead three in silver finish and the other three camouflaged. *M. J. F. Bowyer*

Below:
No 56 Squadron Swift F1s start up at Waterbeach in August 1954. *M. J. F. Bowyer*

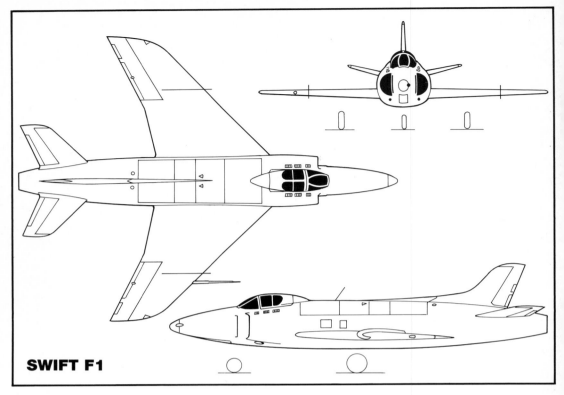

SWIFT F1

May, but WK209 was abandoned in a spin near West Raynham on 7 May and WK208 crashed shortly after take-off on 13 May killing the pilot, Flg Off Thornton, who was on his second flight in the type. This latter crash caused the grounding of the Swifts pending modification of the aileron control system and the rectification of a number of other more minor problems.

The first modified aircraft was test-flown by a Supermarine pilot on 23 July 1954. But inherent problems still existed with the F1s, when the last production aircraft WK213 – the only serviceable aircraft on the squadron – had undercarriage problems on 25 August. Unable to lower his nosewheel, Flg Off Hobbs abandoned the aircraft successfully, landing near Newmarket. All the other Swifts with the squadron were formally grounded.

Meanwhile the F2s were ready to enter service and WK221 and WK240 were delivered to No 56 Squadron on 30 August, with enough arriving by 13 September to allow five to be part of the Battle of Britain flypast over London. By November, serviceability was still very poor, and flying training had to be maintained using Gloster Meteors. There were still hopes that the Swift would make a useful ground attack and reconnaissance aircraft, but on 15 March 1955 the order came to withdraw them from service pending disposal. By early May the surviving aircraft had been flown to No 33 MU at Lyneham for prepara-

tion as ground instruction airframes, pending the eventual re-equipping of No 56 Squadron with Hawker Hunters.

None of the 25 production Swift F3s entered service. The second one, WK248, was used for Controller Aircraft (CA) release handling trials at Boscombe Down in November 1954 and January 1955; WK253 was on service trials at Boscombe Down from February 1955 until October 1956. All the remainder went straight from the production line to ground instruction at various RAF technical training schools.

Top right:
Swift F2, WK240, which was delivered to No 56 Squadron on 30 August 1954, became 7300M in February 1956 for technical training at Halton.
J. M. G. Gradidge

Centre right:
First production Swift F3, WK247, seen here at Farnborough in September 1954, was not issued for service, being used for technical training.
J. M. G. Gradidge

Bottom right:
Swift F3, WK 248, was delivered to Cranfield in December 1957 for technical training.
J. M. G. Gradidge

The F3 was similar to the F2, but the Avon engine was fitted with a reheat. The first example, WK247, was demonstrated at the Farnborough Air Show in September 1953, showing a very lively take-off performance. Pitch up was still a problem, but it had been reduced by fitting vortex generators on upper and lower surfaces of the tailplane.

Amongst the normal trials tasks of the early development F1s, WK198 was converted to the F4 prototype, making its first flight on 27 May 1953. Mike Lithgow flew this prototype to the Paris Show on 5 July 1953 at an average speed of 669.3mph, covering the 212.5 miles in 19min 5.6secs.

The F4 was produced under the Type No 546 and was similar to the F3 but featured a variable incidence tailplane to overcome the pitch-up characteristics. The aircraft appeared to be capable of winning back the Absolute World Speed Record from the USA, and plans were put in hand for the attempt in the latter part of 1953. The ideal climate was located over the deserts of Libya, to enable the aircraft to reach the highest possible speed. The warmer climate gave an increased speed of sound at low level, delaying compressibility and avoiding increased drag. Not only was Libya ideal from the temperature point of view, but there was a well equipped airfield to land at and it was accessible for both the Swift and its support aircraft.

However, before the attempt could be made there was some high priority development flying required, and it was desirable to participate in the SBAC display during the second week in September. This left the record attempt timing towards the end of September, when the temperatures were lowering a little from their summertime peaks. It was still hoped that up to

105°F would be available around mid-afternoon, putting the speed of sound at 790mph. In these conditions it was estimated that the Swift with reheat could reach around 743mph. But Supermarine was not to go unchallenged. Neville Duke, the chief test pilot of Hawker flew the specially prepared red-painted Hunter F3 prototype off the south coast of England to a speed of 729mph, still leaving an adequate margin for the Swift. In the USA plans were also being made for the Douglas Skyray and North American F-100 Super Sabre, both considerably faster than the Swift, to make their attempts on the Absolute World Speed Record.

The Supermarine team left for North Africa on 22 September, a little later than ideal, but still with a good chance of breaking the record before the Americans put it totally out of reach. Despite maintaining a low profile during the initial surveys in Libya, advanced news leaked out at the Farnborough show, largely confirmed by the request for the one and only set of special timing apparatus. The hope had been to find a suitable straight line along the coastline in the vicinity of Tripoli, but the temperature records showed a clear 10°F cooler than just south of Tripoli, and even higher temperatures could be found further inland. Eventually an ideal course was located by the survey party some 50 miles southwest of Tripoli. It was a dead straight main road running for over 10 miles across the Azizia Plain. The only undesirable aspect was the 100 miles from the base airfield, making a return difficult if engine trouble occurred. A forced landing on the 15ft 9in wide road would have been a very challenging operation on the 15ft wide main undercarriage track of the Swift.

The survey of the course was undertaken by the Ordnance Survey of Great Britain and considerable help was given by the RAE Farnborough, which seconded Sqn Ldr John Harvey. The Ordnance Survey team guaranteed the 3km course to an accuracy of 3mm, and a further kilometre was marked out at each end over which the aircraft needed to be in level flight.

Below:
The fifth production Swift, WK198, became the prototype F4, the ultimate Swift fighter variant. It was displayed at Farnborough in September 1953.
J. D. R. Rawlings

A Handley Page Hastings was used to support the record attempt, carrying the timing equipment, the Royal Aero Club observers and the servicing team. The Swift flown by Mike Lithgow, was accompanied by Les Colquhoun in an Attacker, and although the jets arrived in good time, the Hastings was delayed in Marseilles for a day with engine trouble.

The team then began to set up the timing equipment, which had to be mounted on concrete blocks 1,000yds from the side of the road across very difficult terrain. The timing equipment consisted of two pairs of cameras, a pair set up at each end of the course, connected to an electronic timing device. The rules of the record attempt were that the aircraft had to make four runs over the measured course, two in each direction, within a total elapsed time of 30min, during which a landing could be made. At no time from take-off until completion of the fourth run was the aircraft to exceed 1,640ft (500m) altitude, and while over the course the height must not exceed 100m. To help maintain these heights a Gloster Meteor was used to observe one end of the course and an Avro Anson the other end. The Meteor was also used to monitor the take-off and flight to the course of the Swift. The Attacker flying at 5,000ft provided the vital radio communications link.

The first attempt was made on 25 September, but when the fuel gauges ceased to work, Mike Lithgow reduced the reheat time to conserve fuel from an eight-mile approach to the course, to four miles, thus not achieving the full acceleration. The start and finish was indicated by smoke markers on the road, and the turns were made over the desert at about 600mph, climbing to around 1,000ft before making each re-run.

Within four hours of this attempt, the speed was recorded at 737.3mph, later corrected to 735mph due to a camera shutter fault. This speed was felt to be good for a first try, especially taking account of the fuel gauge problem, and the bumpy air turbulence at the time which could reduce the speed by up to 15mph. The next day a second attempt was made, but faults in the timing equipment caused this flight to be void, and spare parts had to be sent out from Britain.

The problem then was to decide to submit the current less than best time as an official record, as if a claim is not made within 48hrs it becomes invalid. Any further attempt, even flown by the same aircraft once claimed, must exceed the previous record by one percent, which would mean exceeding 745mph. If a claim was not made, the lowering temperature in the desert might mean losing the chance of even achieving the figure reached so far. It was therefore decided to submit the claim, but make further runs to improve the previous figures, even though they would not be valid for the record. On one of these attempts 743mph was averaged on the first two runs, but when the reheat failed to ignite on the third run, the sortie was aborted. Soon after, a desert wind blew up making visibility too bad to continue flying, and while waiting for this to die down, the Skyray pushed the record to over 753mph, well out of reach of the Swift.

The Supermarine team then returned home having achieved the Absolute World Speed Record, for only a short period, in a production standard aircraft operating in tropical conditions, demonstrating high performance and long endurance in the most demanding conditions.

In the event only nine Swift F4s were built, of which five were converted to FR5 standard leading to production of 89 of this fighter reconnaissance version of the Swift. A further 11 FR5s were cancelled.

Having had its earlier operational problems corrected, the Swift was not adopted as a fighter due to the lessening of international tension following the end of the Korean conflict. The Hunter was in full production and in widespread squadron service, and there

Below:
Swift F4 prototype, WK198, is prepared for its attempt on the World Absolute Speed Record at El Adem. *RAF Museum*

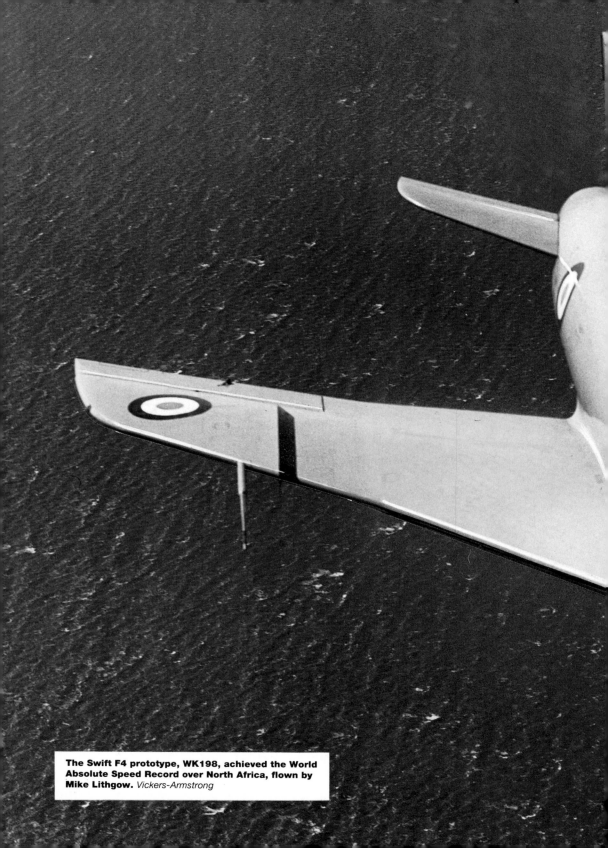

The Swift F4 prototype, WK198, achieved the World Absolute Speed Record over North Africa, flown by **Mike Lithgow.** *Vickers-Armstrong*

Above:
Swift F4, WK275, was used for engine noise trials at Hatfield in the mid-1960s, and is now preserved at Upperhill. *P. J. Birtles*

just was not the need for yet another day fighter, even though the Swift had a higher speed and a greater endurance. Service entry of the Hunter had not been without problems, particularly in respect of the Avon engine which surged when the guns were fired. This was overcome in the short term by fitting the Armstrong Siddeley Sapphire engine to some versions.

The Swift, however, was still capable of making a valuable contribution in the fighter reconnaissance role, to replace the outdated Meteor FR9s. As the Type 549, the FR5 was basically a F4 with a lengthened nose housing three cameras. One was mounted in the extreme nose, and the other two were used for oblique photography and mounted on either side of the nose, a short distance in front of the air intake.

One of the surviving development Swift Mk 1s, WK200, was converted to the prototype FR5 and

undertook service trials at Boscombe Down in July 1953. This aircraft was finally scrapped at Bicester three years later. The first production FR5, XD903 made its maiden flight in the hands of Les Colquhour on 27 May 1955, the next two aircraft having improved clear view canopies and 220gal drop tanks taking fuel capacity to 998gal. The previous F4s WK281, WK287 to 315, and WN124, were all converted to FR5s before issue to the RAF. Swift FR5 production went from XD903 to XD930, and XD948 to XD977. The final batch from XD978 to XD988 were cancelled. The Type 550 unarmed Swift PR6 was proposed to replace the Meteor PR10s, but although XD943 was the first airframe allocated to this task, development was abandoned and the aircraft was not completed.

Below:
Swift F4, WK273, is pictured at Farnborough in September 1954 with eight rocket projectiles under the port wing. *M. J. F. Bowyer*

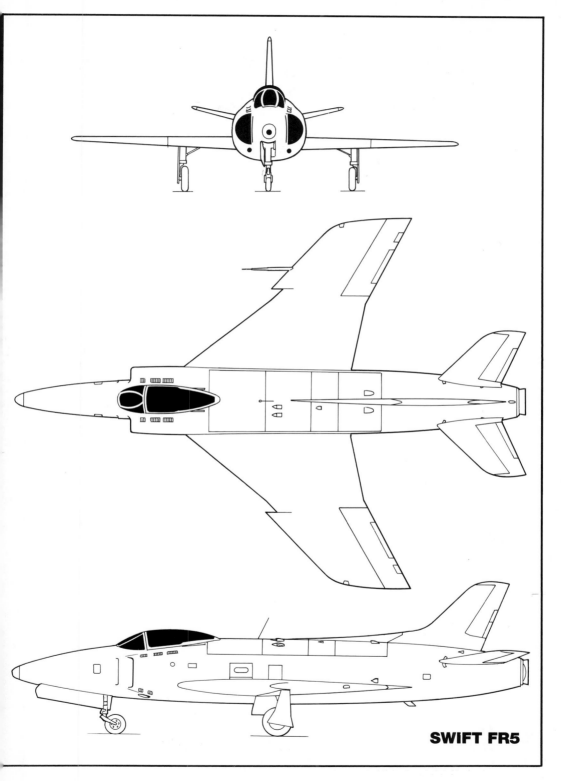

SWIFT FR5

Top left:
Camera installation in prototype Swift FR5 at Chilbolton. Cameras were located in the extreme nose and just forward of the engine air bleed intake. *Supermarine*

Centre left:
Swift FR5, WK296, at Farnborough in September 1956. *M. P. Marsh*

Bottom left:
Swift FR5, XD969, at Aldergrove Battle of Britain show in September 1957. *Tom Crossett*

Below:
Swift FR5, XD916, which was delivered to No 2 Squadron, RAF Germany, in February 1956. *Air Ministry*

Bottom:
Swift FR5, XD962:J of No 2 Squadron, RAF, visited Biggin Hill for the Battle of Britain display in September 1960. *J. M. G. Gradidge*

The Swift FR5 was the first aircraft in RAF service to be equipped with reheat, when in January 1956 No 2 Squadron of the 2nd Tactical Air Force (2TAF) in Germany began to take deliveries at its Geilenkirchen base. In October 1957 a move was made to Jever and the Swifts were gradually replaced by Hunter FR10s from April 1961. No 79 Squadron commenced receiving Swift RF5s at Gütersloh in 1956, also as part of the 2TAF, and continued fighter reconnaissance duties alongside No 2 Squadron. No 79 Squadron was disbanded on 1 January 1961 when it was absorbed into No 4 Squadron to be equipped with Hunter FR10s. While re-equipping with Hunters, No 4 Squadron continued to operate briefly Swift FR5s, some of the aircraft carrying the markings of both the old and the new unit.

Two Swifts of No 79 Squadron had gained first and second places in the NATO Annual Reconnaissance Competition, 'Royal Flush', held at Laarbruch,

Top:
Swift FR5, WK295:G of No 2 Squadron, at West Malling in October 1959. *J. D. R. Rawlings*

Above:
Swift FR5, WN124:S of No 2 Squadron, at Bassingbourn in September 1958, crashed just under a year later on 27 August 1959. *J. D. R. Rawlings*

Below:
Visiting Tangmere in September 1957 was Swift FR5, XD912:C of No 2 Squadron. *J. D. R. Rawlings*

Below right:
The other major operator of the Swift FR5 was No 79 Squadron, also in RAF Germany. *MOD*

Below:
Swift FR5, XD949:D of No 2 Squadron was stored at RAF Aldergrove in December 1959. *Tom Crossett*

Below centre:
RAF Aldergrove was the last resting place of many retired Swift FR5s, one being XD959:V of No 2 Squadron, in December 1959. *Tom Crossett*

Below:
Swift FR5, XD949:D of No 2 Squadron was stored at RAF Aldergrove in December 1959. *Tom Crossett*

Below centre:
RAF Aldergrove was the last resting place of many retired Swift FR5s, one being XD959:V of No 2 Squadron, in December 1959. *Tom Crossett*

West Germany, in May 1957. The mission was low level reconnaissance with photographic recording below 500ft covering 260 nautical miles. The competition mainly consisted of RF-84F Thunderjets operated by the Allied air forces. Two years later the Swifts repeated their success.

The fighter reconnaissance Swifts pioneered high speed low level operations under the hostile radar screens. The robust construction of the Swift stood up well to the punishing conditions, and the terrain following techniques developed by the RAE for future combat aircraft were refined using the Swifts in the multi-high g environment. Not only was the Swift fast and with the desired long endurance, but due to the high integrity of the airframe there were no structural failures in this hostile combat regime.

Above:
Swift FR5 XD953:F of No 79 Squadron, from RAF Germany. *MOD*

Top right:
Swift FR5, WK315:P of 79 Squadron. *J. D. R. Rawlings*

Centre right:
Swift FR5, WK309:S of No 79 Squadron, was stored at Aldergrove in December 1959 after retirement from service. *Tom Crossett*

Bottom right:
For a brief period after No 79 Squadron finished operating Swift FR5s, No 4 Squadron flew them for a month in January 1961 at Gutersloh. FR5, WK293, features No 79 Squadron markings on the rear fuselage and No 4 Squadron markings on the nose. *Eric Taylor*

The final version of the Swift was the F7 first proposed in August 1952 as a design study for the aircraft to be able to carry four Blue Sky air-to-air missiles under the wings with radar guidance. These were in addition to the standard fit of four fixed Aden cannon. The radar was accommodated in a lengthened nose and the wingspan was increased to 36.08ft from the original 32.33ft of the earlier marks. Power came from a Rolls-Royce Avon 116 engine uprated to 7,550lb thrust and F4 WK279 was modified as an aerodynamic prototype. It was fitted with detachable launchers for the missiles and successfully fired three in October 1955.

The first pre-production F7s were XF774, first flown in April 1956, followed by XF778 in June, both used for development flying. The first full production aircraft of a total of 12, XF113, flew in August 1956, and these three aircraft, plus the development prototype were delivered to Boscombe Down for handling and performance trials. With missiles carried under the wings maximum speed was restricted to 580kts or Mach 0.92 up to 20,000ft. The two pre-production prototypes then went to RAF Valley for firing trials, XF778 being fitted with cameras in the nose to record firings from the radar equipped XF774. Ten of the production batch, XF115 to XF124 were allocated to No 1 Guided Weapons Development Squadron (GWDS) at RAF Valley to be the first British fighters

to be equipped with guided missiles in service. The Blue Sky missile was renamed the Fairey Fireflash, and was in fact a radar beam-riding unpowered dart with a high explosive impact warhead. The missiles were accelerated to Mach 2 after launch by a pair of jettisonable booster motors. Although these missiles never entered full operational service, 300 were issued to No 1 GWDS for operational development firings at targets over Cardigan Bay. When these trials were completed the aircraft were retired and scrapped.

The remaining two aircraft did not participate in the weapons trials, XF113 being flown by the Handling Squadron at Boscombe Down in 1956, and then becoming part of the Empire Test Pilots' School (ETPS) fleet at Farnborough until retirement in early 1962. The other aircraft, XF114, was used by Bristol Siddeley Engines at Filton and then with the main undercarriage doors removed was used for wet runway trials at Filton, Heathrow, Upper Heyford and Cranfield in mid-1962 to check the aquaplaning characteristics of various runway surfaces. During this time it was painted overall black and after retirement was

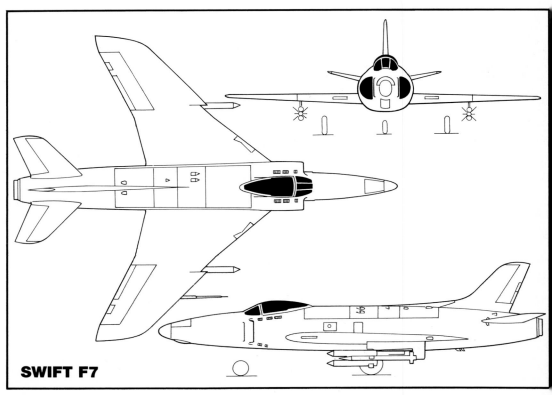

SWIFT F7

delivered by road to Flint Technical College on 24 April 1967 for technical training, still without its main undercarriage doors. It survived for many years and was recovered in excellent condition in early 1989 by Jet Heritage at Hurn Airport. Currently, it is being rebuilt to flying condition, making this the last flying example of any of the Supermarine jet fighters.

The Swift came in for more than its fair share of criticism during its development and service, some of it unjustified. However, it achieved a number of firsts, particularly in its later versions, and became a popular and effective aircraft.

Below:
Swift FR7, XF119, pictured here whilst in service with the Guided Weapons Missile Development Squadron at Valley, carrying underwing Fairey Fireflash beam-riding air-to-air missiles.

6

Twin-Engine Developments

In the early days of jet engine development, the lower power of the engines encouraged the designers to reduce drag and unnecessary weight wherever possible. One aspect looked at by both Britain and France was the operation of aircraft without an undercarriage. The French line of development was the Sud-Barouder, a single-engined lightweight fighter which used a trolley for take-off and skids for landing, the aim being an independence from airfields and long runways. In Britain, however, the approach was to use a flexible deck, dispensing with the weight and complexity of the normal undercarriage, and the problems of stowage in thin wings, and land the aircraft on its belly on a rubber carpet.

Initial trials of the flexible deck were undertaken by Capt Eric Brown using specially adapted Vampire fighters, starting at Farnborough where the first attempt caused considerable damage, but eventually proving the concept as practical in a series of 40 landings. Not only was the plan to use the flexible deck on aircraft carriers, but also site it on land to provide quick landing strips close to the battle zone. The major weakness was of course the lack of mobility on the ground, and the probability of damage to the underside of the aircraft.

It was for this task that the Supermarine twin-jet development was originally planned with a heavy twin Avon-engined Type 505. Once landed on the carpet, the take-off for the next sortie would be catapult-assisted. The side-by-side engine installation ensured a flat cross-section underside for greater stability on landing, and the absence of a main undercarriage allowed a seven percent thickness chord ratio straight wing giving performance improvements in speed and climb rate.

The Type 505 was being designed in 1945 when little was known about swept wings, so a straight wing with a symmetrical section constant over the whole span was provided to avoid tip stalling. The leading edge radius was as large as possible to prevent early airflow breakaway.

To reduce high speed interference effects and drag, a butterfly V-tail was chosen to achieve the required strength for its relatively thin surfaces, and to clear the jet efflux. Pitch control was effected by an all-flying tail, the elevators giving additional control, and rudder movements was replaced by differential movement of the elevators. Lift spoilers were fitted to increase drag

on the approach and dive flaps assisted recovery from high Mach numbers. A lightweight fixed tricycle undercarriage was to be fitted during the initial testing of flight characteristics.

When the Admiralty abandoned the undercarriage-less schemes in 1947, Supermarine adapted its design to the Type 508 fitted with a conventional tricycle retractable undercarriage, and increased the thickness of the wing to nine percent to accommodate it in the stowed position. All-round dimensions were increased to reduce landing speed, the thicker wing also benefiting low level performance and landing characteristics. Wing area was increased from 270 to 310sq ft.

With this all-round increase in size, the Supermarine 508, by now designed to Specification N.9/47, had become the heaviest and most powerful aircraft ever built for the Royal Navy.

Three prototypes were ordered, the first and third to be fully instrumented for experimental flying and the second aircraft allocated to service trials, fitted with the new 30mm cannons under the forward fuselage and radar-ranging mounted in the extreme nose. In addition to a camera gun in a fairing under the nose cone, two vertical and one oblique camera were fitted for fighter reconnaissance duties. The first two prototypes were powered by two Rolls-Royce RA3 Avon engines, each delivering 6,500lb thrust.

The first prototype Type 508, VX133, was transported by road to Boscombe Down, from where Mike Lithgow made the maiden flight on 31 August 1951. The aircraft logged 10 flying hours in time to qualify for an appearance at that year's Farnborough Air Show, where its display was restrained so as not to risk a new unknown type. As later experience was to show, it was perhaps fortunate that the manoeuvres were modest.

Top right:
The Supermarine Type 508, VX113, which first flew on 31 August 1951, was demonstrated at Farnborough one month later. *J. D. R. Rawlings*

Centre right:
The prototype Type 508, VX133, during its development test programme at Chilbolton. *Vickers*

Bottom right:
The Type 508, VX133, flies past the control tower at Chilbolton. *Vickers*

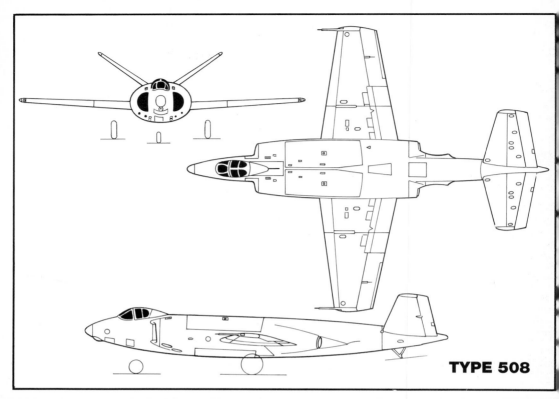

TYPE 508

To provide additional lift for deck landings, the leading edges of the wings automatically drooped when a certain degree of flap was selected. At the same time the ailerons also dropped to form a good low-speed section. Controls were still operated aerodynamically rather than fully powered, which resulted in some undesirable incidents with the Type 508.

The first was when Mike Lithgow was flying the aircraft on 5 December 1951, at low altitude and a speed well below the maximum. For no apparent reason the aircraft began to vibrate violently with no indication of the cause. A very strong uncontrollable nose-up pitch developed, and to attempt to regain control the pilot disengaged the elevator power. This however made things a lot worse and Mike Lithgow blacked out due to the high g forces, regaining consciousness in an upward vertical role at 11,000ft. Control was regained and the accelerometer showed a maximum of 11g which had caused some minor structural damage including loss of both wingtip pitot heads, resulting in no airspeed indication. The return to Chilbolton was made very carefully to avoid any further strain on the overloaded airframe.

Left:
The Type 508, VX133, seen during deck trials on HMS Eagle, 28 May 1952. *FAA Museum*

Top:
The Supermarine Type 529, VX136, was fitted with dorsal strakes ahead of the butterfly tail. *MOS*

Above:
The Supermarine Type 529, VX136, was demonstrated at Farnborough in September 1952. It was intended to equip the aircraft with gun-ranging radar in the nose and a radar warning device in the tail. *J. D. R. Rawlings*

It was assumed during the subsequent investigation that for some reason, the undercarriage had come down in flight. The aircraft was repaired and the undercarriage modified to avoid an inadvertent lowering before it returned to its flight development tasks. A few flights later the same thing happened, but at least the undercarriage stayed up. Also, the incident was viewed from the ground and it was established that aileron flutter caused the problem. The use of power controls overcame this problem, and the Type 508 was otherwise a trouble free aircraft, achieving all its design targets.

On completion of its flight trials the aircraft, with its outer folding wing panels removed, was used by the School of Aircraft Handling at RNAS Culdrose to teach deck handling techniques. It was then relegated to fire practice and was burnt beyond repair before it was realised it might have been worthy of preservation.

The second prototype, VX136, was sufficiently different in detail and armament from the first, to be allocated the new Type 529. It made its first flight almost a year after the first on 29 August 1952, with four 30mm cannon fitted in pairs below the engine intakes. It was planned to install small radomes in the nose for radar ranging, and the tail for tail warning radar, but neither were fitted due to development delays. The Mk 5 gyro gunsight was also withdrawn, so that the aircraft was never used for its planned service trials, although it was not planned to put the aircraft into production. Both the first and second aircraft were deployed on carrier trials where their take-off and climb performance was found to be excellent.

During flight trials both aircraft were found to be prone to flutter which put limitations on their use, but they did provide useful data in operating large and powerful aircraft on carrier decks in preparation for what was due to emerge in the future.

The Type 529 was delivered to the RN test squadron at RAE Bedford on 15 April 1953 for tail-down landing trials, culminating in slight damage in a forced landing on 5 May. The aircraft was soon

Below:
The Type 529, VX136, with folding wings on HMS *Eagle*, 5 November 1953, for deck trials. *FAA Museum*

repaired and commenced catapult acceleration trials in mid-June. The Bedford trials were completed in November, when the aircraft returned to Supermarine at Chilbolton for further development flying, but it was damaged again on 19 December 1953 during an emergency landing.

The aircraft was stored pending a decision on its future, but repair was considered uneconomic with the more representative Type 525 becoming available. The Type 529 was therefore struck off charge on 27 October, 1954 and the major components finally were delivered to the Proof and Explosives Establishment on 29 June 1956 to be used for damage assessment of gunfire on aircraft structures.

The third prototype of the trio of research aircraft, VX138, differed considerably from the earlier two and was designated the Type 525. The major difference between this and earlier aircraft was that the wings and tail surfaces were all swept back, the fin and tailplane being of more conventional cruciform design. It bore an overall similarity to the eventual production aircraft, which in effect was a complete redesign. Despite the major differences, this aircraft was still included in the original specification and higher power came from a pair of Rolls-Royce RA7 Avon engines with a thrust of 7,500lb. Provision was made to fit a reheat RA7R, but this never took place.

Following construction by Supermarine, the aircraft was dismantled and taken by road to Boscombe

Right:

The swept-wing Supermarine Type 525, VX138, was fitted with generous flaps on the wings and under the fuselage. *M. J. F. Bowyer*

Down where Mike Lithgow made the first flight on 27 April 1954. The aircraft was fitted with a sting-type arrester hook in the tail cone, and the fin leading edge area was increased early in the flight trials to improve directional stability.

Supermarine experienced the same basic aerodynamic problems found in the USA with the second generation jet aircraft. Despite the swept surfaces and more powerful engines, there was only a very modest increase in speed, as the area rule was not applied. This allowed for a smooth curve if the overall cross section was plotted, but if the wings gave a sharp increase in the cross-sectional area, the speed would be limited. The familiar waisted or 'Coke bottle' effect overcame this problem. Therefore although it was then probably the most powerful swept wing aircraft in the world, it could only just exceed the speed of sound in a dive. This basic shortcoming was corrected in the design of the Type 544, destined to become the production Scimitar.

The Type 525 was fitted with a taller undercarriage positioned further out on the wings and the overall length was 52ft due to the swept back tail surfaces. To allow practical carrier operations, high lift devices were essential for approach and landing. The Type 525 had NACA double-slotted flaps on the wing trailing edge, joined by extensions under the fuselage, and tapered leading edge slots from wing root to tip. In addition, lift spoilers, Attacker-type air brakes and dive recovery flaps were provided as part of the complex control systems.

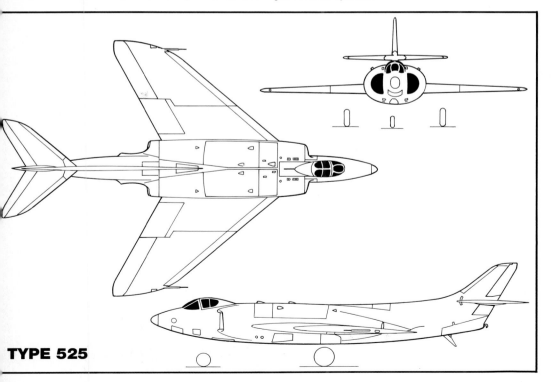

TYPE 525

Top:
The swept-wing and tail Type 525, VX138, led to the development of the Scimitar. *Vickers*

Above:
Type 525, VX138, seen at Farnborough on 8 September 1954.
J. D. R. Rawlings

A swept butterfly tail had been originally proposed, with variable incidence through a hinged tail cone, but structural considerations resulted in the more conventional design.

As a further part of the programme to improve handling on the approach to landing, Supermarine developed its experience of laminar flow. The surplus of air available from the compressors of the more powerful jet engines coming into service would allow the boundary layer turbulence to be overcome by sucking or blowing through perforations in the aerofoil surfaces. Supermarine developed a flap blowing system for the Type 525, which projected a thin jet of high pressure air through a narrow slot along the wing trailing edge, just ahead of the flap hinge. This jet of air tended to follow the contour of the flap when it was deflected, avoiding the turbulence caused by the boundary layer separation and rapid rise of drag. As a result the approach speed was reduced by some 18mph and the smaller angle of attack gave an improved view for the pilot on the approach. Control and stability was significantly improved at lower speeds because of a smoother wake and more stable airflow over the trailing edges.

A denavalised version of the Type 525, designated the Type 526, was offered to RAF Specification F.3/48 but was not adopted. A tandem seat trainer version was considered, still with a swept butterfly tailplane, as the Type 539.

The Type 525, painted in a gloss cream overall colour scheme, participated in the September 1954 SBAC display at Farnborough, but on 5 July 1955 it was totally destroyed in a fatal crash following an uncontrolled spin, ending the era of twin-jet experimental design, which paved the way for an effective production programme.

7

The Scimitar

As a logical development of the Type 525, the Type 544 was produced, known initially as the N113, before becoming the Scimitar for the FAA. This was to be the last in a long line of Supermarine aircraft, the name being absorbed fully into Vickers when that company became part of the British Aircraft Corporation.

The first prototype N113, WT854, made its initial flight with Mike Lithgow from Boscombe Down on 19 January 1956, followed by two more prototypes, WT895 and WW134 in the same year. The third prototype was the first aircraft to be fitted with blown flaps. Deck trials were flown with the first prototype in April 1956 from HMS *Ark Royal*, with further deck trials flown in January 1957 using the more representative third prototype.

Changing operational requirements caused the Scimitar to shift its designated role from single-seat fighter to a low level strike aircraft capable of using the below radar coverage Low Altitude Bombing System (LABS) attack method. In addition, the aircraft would be capable of launching a tactical nuclear device, all with a single pilot as crew and modest radar for weapon sighting. The overall design had complied with the area rule, giving the N113 a supersonic capability in a shallow dive, the high speed being helpful in departing from a hostile environment. The airframe

therefore was of robust construction to withstand the heavy flight loads and gusts at high speed and low altitude, especially when pulling high g manoeuvres.

With the high subsonic speeds at which the Scimitar would be expected to operate, effective control was a major problem to overcome. This generation of high speed aircraft was experiencing a pitch-up in longitudinal control apparent at high altitude and high Mach numbers. This unwelcome characteristic was caused by the sonic shock wave-induced separation of the air flow over the wing, leading to a high speed tip stall, aggravated by the increased downwash over the all-flying tailplane, without its own elevators. The solution to the problem was to introduce saw tooth notches in the wing leading edge together with boundary layer fences and Kuchemann-shaped flared out wingtips. This worked for many of the contemporary swept wing jet fighters of the time, but the N113 benefited as much as anything from converting the tailplane from a ten degree dihedral to a ten degree anhedral.

Below:
The strop drops away as one of the N113 D prototypes climbs away from HMS *Ark Royal* at deck trials in 1957. *Vickers*

Above:
Supermarine N113, WT854, with the original dihedral tailplane on arrester trials at RAE Bedford. *Vickers*

Below:
Supermarine N113, WT854, prototype for the Scimitar, seen at Farnborough in September 1956 after the anhedral tailplane had been fitted.
J. M. G. Gradidge

The rate of roll was very high at moderate Mach numbers, and the ailerons tended to be oversensitive. The N113 was the first British naval aircraft to use duplicated power controls, the required accuracy being achieved by adding supplementary hydraulic jacks to the original Fairey power controls, and introducing differential gearing to produce the finer degree of accuracy required.

A concern of the Supermarine design team was the inertia forces generated during rapid rolls, particularly during roll pull-outs, which could induce excessive yaw. This could cause structural damage to an aircraft of the N113 layout with short lightweight wings and a

Below left:
The somewhat battered N113 Scimitar prototype, WT854, in use at RNAS Culdrose in 1970 for training ground handlers. *J. D. R. Rawlings*

Below:
Third prototype N113, WW134, with blown flaps aboard HMS *Ark Royal* for deck trials in early 1957, with 'C' Squadron at Boscombe Down. *Supermarine*

Above:
Supermarine N113 second prototype, WT859, still with the dihedral tailplane. *Vickers*

heavy long fuselage. The computer studies confirmed that the strength contingency allowance provided by the advanced engineering would cope with any problems of this nature.

To withstand the high loads on the structure, high-tensile steel was used for the main wing spars, and for areas of major stress in the wing and tail. Titanium was used in lower stress areas where heat resistance was required. To overcome acoustic damage by the engine jet efflux on rear fuselage panels, thicker skins were mounted on steel ribs, bonded with a synthetic resin backed by a foam filling. The majority of the remainder of the airframe was conventional light alloy structure with the skins chemically milled to reduce weight where appropriate. An overall fatigue life of 1,000hrs was achieved, an average for high performance military aircraft, but hardly acceptable in commercial aircraft.

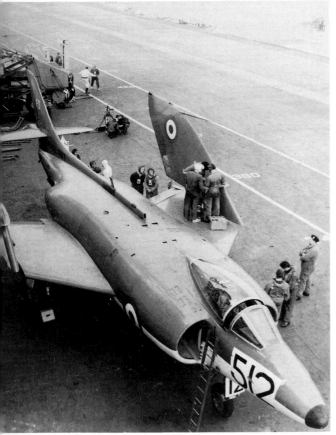

Above:
XD212 was the first production Scimitar F1. *Vickers*

Left:
Scimitar F1:512/FD of 700(X) Squadron, FAA, during deck service trials. *FAA Museum*

The Scimitar was the largest, heaviest and most powerful single-seat jet fighter to serve with the Fleet Air Arm and was complementary to the two-seat de Havilland Sea Vixen all-weather fighter.

As mentioned earlier, the prototype WT854 made the initial deck landing trials on HMS *Ark Royal*, following a series of simulated deck landings on an arrester gear-equipped runway at RAE Bedford. By November 1957 a total of 148 deck landings and catapult take-offs had been achieved, giving an ideal approach speed of 124kt at a landing weight of 28,000lb. To achieve this, flap blowing was used giving a steeper attitude on the approach, and improving the pilot's view over the nose. The maximum permissible weight for a steam catapult launch was 34,000lb.

The first production Scimitar, XD212, made its maiden flight on 11 January 1957 and shared development with a number of the early batch of aircraft. This included Bullpup missile trials, acceptance trials at Boscombe Down and HMS *Ark Royal*, and the forming of 700X Flight for operational trials. Initial deck training was carried out at Boscombe Down, and the formation of 700X Flight was an innovation for the introduction of a complex weapons system, to determine the best ways to operate the new aircraft in a realistic service environment.

Above:
The Scimitar was introduced to FAA service with 700 Squadron at RNAS Ford from August 1957 to June 1958. XD220:511 of 700 Squadron is prepared for flight in June 1958. *J. D. R. Rawlings*

Left:
No 803 Squadron Scimitars, XD242:152N, and XD230:151/V, ready for catapult departure from HMS *Victorious.* *FAA Museum*

Below left:
Scimitar F1, XD264:154/V of 803 Squadron, aboard the HMS *Victorious.* *RAF Museum/Cyril Peckham*

700X Flight formed at RNAS Ford on 27 August 1957 commanded by Cdr T. G. Innes, receiving its first Scimitar in May 1958. It continued with the operational development task until February 1959. Meanwhile, 803 FAA Squadron commenced operational training at Lossiemouth on 3 June 1958, as the first frontline squadron under the command of Cdr J. D. Russell. The eight Scimitar F1s embarked on HMS *Victorious* in September, working up in home waters before spending a few weeks in the Mediterranean Sea towards the end of 1959.

Much of the following year was spent ashore based at Lossiemouth, re-embarking on HMS *Victorious* in October for a further period in the Mediterranean, including 10 days on shore at Hal Far in Malta. A return was made to Lossiemouth on 19 December to prepare for Far Eastern service for a duration of 10 months. The departure was made on HMS *Victorious* in January 1961, reaching Tengah in Singapore two months later. While afloat, a visit was made to Butter-

79

No 803 Squadron, FAA, Scimitars aboard HMS _Victorious_, with Sea Vixens and Gannets. _FAA Museum_

worth in Malaya for a month in the summer, testing the operation of the Scimitar in the full range of hot weather climates. The squadron departed the area on 5 October 1961, arriving back at Lossiemouth via Yeovilton on 9 December.

On 25 May 1962, 803 Squadron transferred to HMS *Hermes*, returning to the Mediterranean until October when a month was spent in preparation for a further tour of the Far East on HMS *Hermes*, which was to become the 803 Squadron floating base for a couple of years. During this tour from November 1962 until October 1963, further shore detachments were made at Tengah. In February 1964 the strength of the squadron was doubled to 16 aircraft when 803

Above left:
Scimitar F1, XD268: 156/V 803 Squadron, FAA, is about to take off from the Farnborough runway. *M. J .F. Bowyer*

Left:
Scimitar F1, XD231:152/V of 803 Squadron, from HMS *Victorious* at RNAS Ford in June 1958. *M. J. F. Bowyer*

Top:
Scimitar F1, XD267, of 803 Squadron at Lossiemouth in April 1964. *J. D. R. Rawlings*

Above:
Scimitar F1 of 803 Squadron is about to leave the deck of HMS *Ark Royal* with the assistance of the steam catapult.

absorbed the disbanded 800 Squadron. No 803 Squadron spent much of the year at its Lossiemouth base, with detachments south to Yeovilton. Eight aircraft from 803 Squadron participated in the service contribution to the Farnborough Air Show in September 1964, sharing the FAA limelight with Sea Vixens and Wessex. In December its allocated ship became HMS *Ark Royal*. After work-up on this carrier in January, 803 departed in June, once more for the Far East, where Changi in Singapore and Butterworth were the land bases. Amongst the operational duties were two spells on the Beira patrol before returning to Lossiemouth and disbanding on 1 October 1966.

Above:
No 803 Squadron Scimitar F1, fitted with underwing 'buddy' refuelling pod, is ready for catapult take-off from HMS *Ark Royal*.

Below:
In May 1964, the FAA celebrated its 60th anniversary with a review at Yeovilton. Scimitar XD235:149/R of 803 Squadron was part of the line-up of representative serving aircraft. *P. J. Birtles*

Bottom:
Scimitar F1, XD276, of 803 Squadron at the point of touchdown on HMS *Ark Royal*, in May 1965.
J. D. R. Rawlings

Right:

Scimitar F1, XD325, of 803 Squadron picks up the arrester wire on HMS *Ark Royal* in May 1965. *J. D. R. Rawlings*

Below:

The moment of truth! Scimitar F1 XD333:150/R of 803 Squadron prepares to leave the deck of HMS *Ark Royal* in May 1965. *J. D. R. Rawlings*

Bottom:

After service with 803 Squadron, Scimitar XD276 served on ground instruction duties at RNAS Lee-on-Solent where it was put in the static display for a Navy Day in June 1968. *P. J. Birtles*

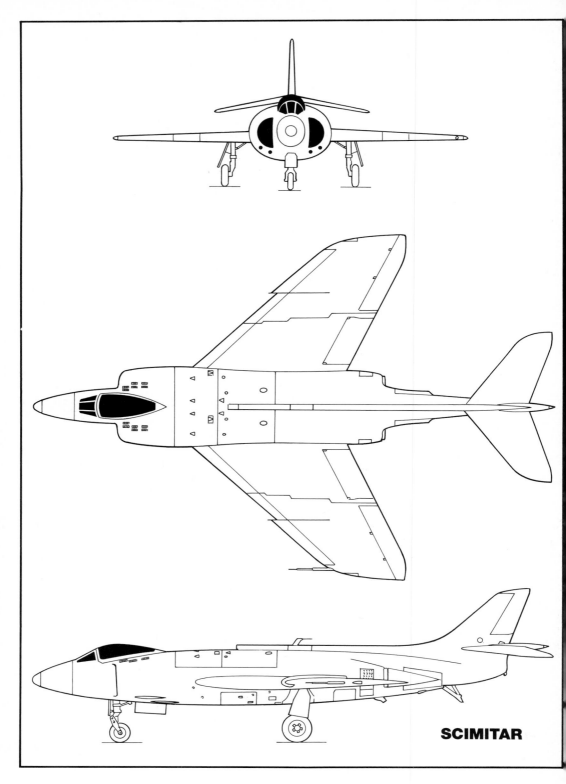

SCIMITAR

As well as being able to fire Bullpup missiles in the air-to-ground role, the Scimitar could also carry the Sidewinder air-to-air missile, unguided rocket projectiles, four 1,000lb bombs or four 200gal drop tanks. Fixed armament was four 30mm Aden cannon and the aircraft could carry a flight refuelling 'buddy' pack to support other Scimitars.

The Scimitar operational training task was undertaken by 736 Squadron based at Lossiemouth from June 1959 until March 1965, when it took over Buccaneer training. The duty of the squadron was to train pilots to frontline standard, providing them with experience in photo reconnaissance and ground-attack using bombs, rockets, guns and Bullpup missiles, Sidewinder air-to-air interceptions, low level navigation and army cooperation. Five Scimitars from the 736 Squadron aerobatic team performed at the Farnborough Air Show in September 1962, often flying close to the now banned Mach 1 and doing a formation quartet 'twinkle' roll, now more famous with the Red Arrows. Following its disbandment as a Scimitar training unit, this task was taken over by 764 (B) Squadron for a couple of months, before Hawker Hunter T8s took on Air Warfare Instructor training.

Top left:
Scimitar F1 XD239:613 of 736 Squadron visited the Wethersfield air show in May 1962 carrying Sidewinder air-to-air missiles on underwing pylons. M. J. F. Bowyer

Centre left:
Early production Scimitar F1 XD215:611 of 736 Squadron appeared at the Biggin Hill Air Fair in May 1965, carrying dummy 250lb bombs and fuel drop tanks under the wings. J. M. G. Gradidge

Bottom left:
At Farnborough Air Show in September 1962, 736 Squadron participated with its Scimitars within the Royal Navy set piece. XD219 is seen on the point of landing alongside another Scimitar. M. J. F. Bowyer

Top:
Scimitar F1, XD332:612 of 736 Squadron at Lossiemouth, the home of the Scimitar units, in August 1966. J. D. R. Rawlings

Above:
No 736 Squadron Scimitar F1, XD224, at Lossiemouth in 1960 before the tail markings were adopted. R. C. B. Ashworth

Above:
The 807 Squadron, FAA, Scimitar aerobatic team practises near Invergerdon whilst operating from Lossiemouth. *FAA Museum*

The second Scimitar frontline unit was 807 which recommissioned on 1 October 1958 at RNAS Lossiemouth with eight aircraft. It remained on shore working up to operational status until March 1960 when it embarked on HMS *Ark Royal* for a tour in the Mediterranean. During the work-up period the squadron introduced the Scimitar to the public at the SBAC Farnborough Air Show in September 1959. Their demonstration was the finale of the show with four in a box formation and two solos led by Lt-Cdr Leppard. No 807 Squadron's display featured a solo

LABS bombing technique, a high speed target snatch by a hook from the runway, and when the two single-ton Scimitars landed in one direction on the Farnborough runway, they folded their wings to let through another Scimitar landing in the opposite direction. Their tail markings featured a scimitar.

During its tour of duty in the Mediterranean, the aircraft were shore-based at Hal Far and Gibraltar. In April 1961 a transfer was made to HMS *Centaur*, and after a further spell in the Mediterranean, the ship sailed to the Persian Gulf where 807 Squadron helped

Below:
No 807 Squadron, FAA's, Scimitar XD267 is pictured at Farnborough in September 1959. *M. J. F. Bowyer*

to keep the peace in an earlier Gulf crisis when Iraq
was threatening Kuwait. In August, the Scimitars
returned to Lossiemouth via Malta to prepare for a Far
East tour on HMS *Centaur* commencing in October
1961. On the return home from this tour, some time
was spent at Malta, before finally flying to
Lossiemouth and disbanding on 15 May 1962.

No 800 Squadron received its first of eight Scimitars on 1 July 1959 at Lossiemouth under the command of Lt-Cdr Norman. After working up at its home
base the squadron embarked on HMS *Ark Royal*, passing through the Mediterranean with detachments at
Hal Far, en route to the Far East. Here it spent a number of detachments at Tengah before returning to
Lossiemouth to be absorbed into 803 Squadron on
25 February 1964. During one of its home base
deployments, 800 Squadron combined with the Scimitars of 804 Squadron at the SBAC Farnborough Air
Show in September 1961. No 800 Squadron was rep-
resented by six Scimitars led by Lt-Cdr Danny Norman, supported by three formations from HMS *Hermes* including a formation of five Scimitars and one

Above:
Scimitar F1, XD277 101/R of 800 Squadron, participated at the Farnborough Air Show in September 1961. *J. D. R. Rawlings*

solo aircraft from 804 Squadron. The solo aircraft from 804 Squadron shared a LABS demonstration with a Sea Vixen from 890 Squadron.

The final frontline Scimitar unit was 804 Squadron, already mentioned due to its part in the September SBAC Farnborough Air Show. This squadron only operated the Scimitar for 18 months, from March 1960

until September 1961. The squadron formed at Lossiemouth with six Scimitars on 1 March 1960 and embarked on HMS *Hermes* on 6 July for a work-up, prior to being stationed in the Far East with its land base at Tengah, Singapore. A return was made to Lossiemouth in April 1961, and following more work with HMS *Hermes* in home waters, the squadron was disbanded on 15 September.

Below:
Nine Scimitars of 800 Squadron were part of the Royal Navy contribution to the Farnborough Air Show in September 1961. *J. M. G. Gradidge*

The Scimitar was withdrawn from frontline service at its home base at Lossiemouth when 803 Squadron disbanded in October 1966, in preparation to receive the replacement two-seat radar-equipped Buccaneers.

A total of 76 production Scimitars had been built at South Marston, the last being delivered in September 1960. A further batch of 24 aircraft had been cancelled.

Following the retirement of the Scimitar from service, a number of the aircraft were put into storage at

Above:
Following its service with 800 (B) Squadron, Scimitar F1 XD243 was issued to RNAS Lee-on-Solent for technical training where it was used in the air day static park in June 1968. *P. J. Birtles*

Below:
Rarely photographed Scimitars of 804 Squadron, FAA, for example XD325:163/H from HMS *Hermes*. *FAA Museum*

Brawdy pending their release to Airwork FRU at Hurn Airport. Others were allocated to ground trials or training work, consisting of aquaplaning research at Farnborough with XD219 with the outer wings removed, carrier deck handling training, and gunfire damage assessment at Foulness.

Airwork operated the Scimitar on Fleet Requirements duties from December 1965 to December 1970 when the aircraft were finally withdrawn from flying duties.

The Scimitar was, therefore, the last in a long and illustrious line of Supermarine single-seat high performance aircraft, from the world-beating Schneider Trophy racers, to the war-winning Spitfire and the pioneering jet fighters. A truly proud heritage for such a modest company.

Above:
During the latter days of its service, RNAS Brawdy was used as a holding unit, where Scimitar F1, XD321, was stored in September 1957. *P. J. Birtles*

Below:
The ultimate user of the Scimitar on flying duties was the Airwork FRU at Hurn, of which XD236 was an example. *J. M. G. Gradidge*

8

Flying the Supermarine Jets Test Flying Impressions by David Morgan

David Morgan, recently retired from British Aerospace, was a development test pilot with Supermarine through the majority of the test programmes on the jet fighters and the associated experimental aircraft.

Dave had served initially in the RAF and then joined the RNVR in 1944 flying Seafires with the FAA. At the end of World War 2 he joined a ferry flying unit before being posted to the Central Flying School at Little Rissington to become a Qualified Flying Instructor. From here he was posted to RNAS Lee-on-Solent to retrain pilots following ground tours, flying Harvards, Seafires and Fireflies. Following his attendance at No 7 Course at the Empire Test Pilots' School, Dave returned to Lee-on-Solent with the Carrier Trials Unit. A feature of the FAA at that time was that appointments tended to be short and it was only six months before a move was made to take over the Naval section of the Handling Squadron at RAF Manby, tasked with the compilation of the pilot's notes for the new aircraft then entering service.

On 2 June 1950 David Morgan joined Supermarine at Chilbolton as a test pilot on the Attacker programme. The design office and experimental hangar were at Hursley Park and the prototypes built there were taken by road to Boscombe Down for the maiden flights. All experimental and development test flying was from Chilbolton, while production and the associated routine test flying was from the South Marston works near Swindon.

When Dave joined Supermarine there were three Attackers on test, the aircraft being basically a Spiteful wing fitted to a jet fuselage. With the loss of the second prototype, TS413, the original prototype was adapted for naval work, as there was no RAF interest in the type. One prototype had larger air intakes and the wing position changed to significantly improve longitudinal control, but the urgency of production called for the original configuration.

The prototype, TS409, was very heavy on the controls fore and aft, particularly at low speeds and production aircraft were heavier. An elevator with flat sides brought about some improvement. The ailerons were also improved by fitting lighter springs to the tabs, reducing forces in the roll.

Production aircraft never flew as well as TS409, probably due to tolerances affecting aerodynamic balancing, although the first production aircraft, WA469, was quite close to the earlier standards. The wings of RN aircraft folded across the mid-span of the ailerons and the RPAF aircraft which did not have this feature were generally more pleasant to fly.

A problem which emerged quite late in the development programme was stalling of the fin when recovering from a flat turn or straight sideslip. Full rudder could be reached in both cases, without any sign of fin stall or rudder overbalance, and normal flight regained by progressively centring the controls. However, a complete release of the controls resulted in the aircraft rearing up and doing one – and sometimes two – violent flick rolls before control was regained. A dorsal fin provided a complete cure.

Dave's first flight in an Attacker was some months before joining Supermarine when he took the opportunity to ferry TS409 from Boscombe Down to Chilbolton. His immediate impression was how much faster it was than a Vampire and how much less 'tense' than a Meteor 8 at 500kts low down. The lift spoilers, designed to facilitate carrier landing were also a great help landing an unfamiliar aircraft on a shortish runway, but manoeuvring at low speeds on the ground was not easy due to the twin tailwheel.

In August 1950, Dave was tasked with taking the prototype Attacker to Pakistan for the Independence Day celebrations. He experienced an electrical fault in Cyprus which necessitated a complete electrical panel being flown out by a civil airline. The panel was then fitted by the RAF squadron's electrician at Nicosia. The next leg to Baghdad ended in a landing with one main undercarriage leg up. Much of the load was taken by the belly tank which was replaced with one brought out by the rescue team who flew straight

Above:
Jeffrey Quill, wartime Spitfire test pilot (left) with David Morgan, preparing to deliver a brace of Attackers to Pakistan. *Supermarine*

through from Weybridge in a Valetta and had the Attacker serviceable in five days. He arrived in time for the Commander-in-Chief, Air Vice-Marshal Atcherley, to lead the flypast in TS409 painted in the colours of the, then, Royal Pakistan Air Force.

For production test flights a calibrated sensitive altimeter was fitted to check the functioning of the cockpit pressurisation system. When climbing through 40,000ft on a normal test flight, Les Colquhoun had the canopy seal explode causing a rapid depressurisation and the calibrated altimeter settled at 42,000ft. It was checked and found to be accurate. It was concluded that the suction generated around the canopy caused the increase in cabin altitude and it made one realise how close one had been to anoxia flying unpressurised aircraft like TS409, not to mention Meteor 7s to heights of 45,000ft breathing oxygen without pressure assistance.

The Supermarine 510 was an Attacker with swept back wings and tail surfaces. It was looked upon as the No 1 sharp aircraft in 1950 and was splendid when flown by Mike Lithgow at the RAF Display at Farnborough that year. The Hawker P1052 was in a similar class to the Type 510, but the American F-86 Sabre was faster at low altitude due to lower drag and a much more efficient intake/engine combination. The Sabre had also exceeded the speed of sound because of its virtually fully-powered ailerons and variable incidence tailplane with a boosted elevator.

After some development work mainly concerned with the power assisted controls, the Type 510 became

the first swept-wing jet aircraft to land on the deck of an aircraft carrier. It was fitted with an arrester hook and rocket assisted take-off gear (RATOG). The trials were flown on HMS *Illustrious* by Mike Lithgow, Chief Test Pilot of Supermarine, Lt-Cdr (Later Rear Admiral) Doug Parker from Boscombe Down and Lt Jock Elliot from Aero Flight Farnborough. The trials revealed no great problems in landing and the only major incident was during a take-off when RATOG on the port side failed to light and the ensuing swing and wing drop brought the wingtip into contact with the ship's forward gun turret. The powerful ailerons enabled the subsequent out-of-trim forces to be held quite easily and the aircraft was flown to Chilbolton and landed safely.

The second Type 510, VV119, had guns built into the wings; it was soon given a nosewheel undercarriage in a lengthened nose, and became the Type 535. It was still powered by the Rolls-Royce Nene engine, initially with reheat, but this was not successful. It was a beautiful looking aeroplane and was first seen publicly at the 1950 SBAC Farnborough Air Show, flown by Mike Lithgow.

The second Type 535, WJ960, was the first to be powered by the Avon RA7 engine, which became the Type 541. Dave Morgan was due to demonstrate the new aircraft at Farnborough in September 1951, while Mike Lithgow flew the larger twin-engined Type 508.

On the Saturday just before the show, Dave was tasked with a high altitude test, followed by a Farnborough practice in WJ960. On completion of the sortie preparation was made for the landing at Chilbolton approaching over the valley in which flowed the River Test. As full flap was selected on final approach, engine power was increased to overcome the extra drag. The RA7 engine suffered a kind of 'flat spot' at this part of the rpm range due to the operation of intake swirl vanes and compressor bleed valves, so one was used to somewhat uneven response to throttle movement. On this occasion, however, there was a loud bang, a vapour cloud around the intakes and an almost complete loss of power.

The Swift was not a very efficient glider under these conditions so the undercarriage was selected 'up' and the flaps set to 'max lift'. Even so, the rapid initial height loss made clear that there was no chance of clearing the ridge which confronted the aircraft, much less gaining the airfield, and a turn to the right was made towards what was more open country. The descent continued and no response to throttle occurred. The intended flight path was now constrained by the ridge on the left and a line of high tension cables converging from the right. There existed some doubt as to the possibility of clearing the cables and the aircraft was pushed down to fly underneath them. There was then little height left and only minimum flying speed and a touch down was expected on the crest of a grass covered slope. When the crest was

Above:

Swift F7, XF114, is seen here at Cranfield in June 1966, with the main undercarriage doors removed, configured for braking trials on wet runways. It was this aircraft which so nearly was bulldozed off the runway at Upper Heyford. Following preservation at Flintshire College, it is now being restored to flying condition at Hurn. *P. J. Birtles*

ached there was a house right on the nose. It was just possible to turn enough to go between the house and the barn but the gap was narrower than the wingspan and some three feet off the port wing were left on their outside privy, built strongly in brick and fortunately unoccupied! On inspecting the approach afterwards, Dave found that the tail pipe had actually dragged on the ground for some 20yds before impact.

The aircraft came to a halt in a stubble field, with the engine still running, which Dave stopped with the low pressure cock (the HP cock linkage having been broken), and rapidly jumped out of the aircraft. He looked into the air intake and saw the starter motor lying in the compressor inlet.

The first person to arrive on the scene was a woman running from the farm, whose comment on arrival at the aircraft was 'Oh dear, we have been expecting something like this to happen. They have been coming over very low recently.' All Dave could suggest was that people should keep away from the scene as there was an explosive ejection seat fitted.

They walked back to Charity Down Farm along the landing path and Dave was surprised to find a group of four or five elderly men sitting down to tea, but nobody looked up when Dave entered and apologised for the disturbance. They did, however, come to life when he produced his cigarettes. Each man took one and laid it carefully by his plate, with one chap saying 'Thank you, I will have just one!'.

Air Traffic at Chilbolton had told Chunky Horne, who was airborne in an Attacker from South Marston, that they had seen the Swift disappear into the Test Valley on the approach to runway 12 and it was not long before Dave heard him fly over, after which he left the tea party. Chunky had spotted the Swift and called the Tower to give directions for the fire truck. Soon other people appeared on the scene, including

Joe Smith, the Chief Designer. He was still running-in his new Humber Super Snipe, the cross country driving not being the best way to treat the new car. The next day Dave took VV119 to Farnborough and flew it in the SBAC Show. WJ960 was flying again within three months.

It was decided to exhibit the Swift prototype at the NATO display in Brussels in June 1952, alongside the Hawker Hunter and the North American F-86 Sabre.

To take full advantage it was also planned to break the London to Brussels speed record. To achieve the maximum speed, one needed to arrive with minimum fuel. Since there was no knowledge of the ultimate range of the aircraft, closed circuit flights were made to determine the endurance. The gallons used were measured against time in the closed circuit at altitudes of 10,000ft, 5,000ft and on the deck. It was established that for the record attempt all the fuel would be used at low level, but that 60gal would remain in the tanks if the aircraft was flown at 10,000ft; for safety the latter was chosen. The start was planned from London-Heathrow airport and a visibility of at least 10 miles was required to pin-point the destination, especially as the approach to Brussels lacked landmarks. Visibility was too bad on the first day, but marginal enough on the second to make an attempt worthwhile. Before departure, however, the BBC reporter recorded both the departure and arrival interview from Dave in anticipation of success.

Departure was by flying down runway 10 left at the required height of 100m and a gentle climb started to 10,000ft, reaching the coast at North Foreland in just six minutes. It was planned to start descending, maintaining speed, about the town of Ghent but a large cumulus cloud caused this to be delayed for about 30sec (5 miles). All other traffic was being held clear of Melsbroek so Dave only had to look for their airport; this came up on the nose at about five miles. The time was just over 18min, an average speed of 666mph. There was just under 100gal of fuel remaining which, in theory, meant that the flight could have been made at a lower altitude and in a faster time. The record was recognised by the FAI and still stands.

The next progression in the development programme was the first Swift F1 prototype, WJ965. This aircraft had a roomy cockpit, 500gal of internal fuel, a new wing position, and new Fairey power controls which were very smooth in operation. Dave made the maiden flight from Boscombe Down of this aircraft, which he found quieter than the previous aircraft. The production Mk 1 aircraft were armed with two 20mm cannons mounted in the fuselage with ammunition in the wing roots. The flaps, as developed on the Type 535, were used as airbrakes and were most effective; however, the change in wing position had introduced a trim change which was not acceptable and early work was aimed at curing this. It was eliminated by 'clipping' the outer end of the flaps and adding to the inboard end; the previous impeccable qualities were then restored.

During the flight-testing programme on WJ965, a vibration started at 520kts which stopped when the engine was throttled back. As the handling programme progressed the vibration built up rapidly at 560kts, blurring the instrument panel, leading to a suspicion that the elevators may be a problem.

However, Dave felt that the problem was more associated with aileron flutter, although other expert opinion suspected aileron 'buzz' which was a high Mach number oscillation.

WJ965 was fitted with instrumentation to trac aileron, elevator and tab operation, with a came recording control surface movement, starting towar the end of 1952. As speed built up, the control colum was banged to excite the aircraft, at high and low alt tudes. At high altitude, the vibration could be stoppe by pulling g, and indicated the need to replace th spring tabs with geared tabs.

At low altitude, the vibration was found to be ver serious; it had not occurred on WJ960, although th wing was claimed to be identical. As speed wa increased from 530kts the vibration built up, th aileron oscillating, but on looking along the wing lea ing edge, Dave could see the whole wingtip flexing an estimated 8 cycles/sec. He drew on his knee-pa the position of where the wing was bending.

Alan Clifton, the Deputy Chief Designer, took th sketch back to Hursley Park to check the drawings ar the resonance testing results. What he found was th for ease of production and lightness, the outer win skins had been made thinner, giving a change of stif ness and causing a different flutter characteristic. E stiffening up the wing structure this was avoided, ar the 'knee-pad' report by Dave turned out to be a ver accurate assessment of one part of the problem.

The other was finally solved by replacing th spring tabs by geared tabs, and although the aircra was less pleasant to fly, flutter was avoided. Dav flew this aircraft in trials to exceed the speed of soun increasing the angle of each dive progressively to se what happened. The aircraft had power boosted co trols and a fixed tailplane, but at high Mach numbe

Below:
Left to right: David Morgan, Alan Clifton, Mike Lithgow, Jeffrey Quill and Alan Greenwood at Wisley in July 1957. *Vickers*

se to Mach 1.0, there was no longitudinal or lateral
ntrol. Pulling the stick back had no effect, but nei-
er did pushing forward. Eventually, having set the
craft into the required angle of dive, Mach 1.0 was
ceeded with hands off the controls, recovery being
throttling back and pulling out at lower altitude
ere the Mach number and speed dropped due to the
nser air.

At about this time the feature film *Sound Barrier*
s being made. This film featured VV119 which had
en flown by Dave. A certain degree of artistic
ence was invoked to depict recovery of control at
eeds around Mach 1 by reversing the control move-
nts, but in all other respects the film was a faithful
rtrayal of events at the time.

The Swift and Hunter were both put into super pri-
ty production, potentially supplying up to 50 air-
ft a month to the RAF. With the end of the Korean
ar, the need was no longer there and the aircraft to
fer from the greatest cuts was the Swift. The air-
ft became a political football and when the first
ifts were delivered to No 56 Squadron at Water-
ach, they had limitations of 25,000ft altitude and top
ed of Mach 0.9. The reason for this was that
scombe had not at that time finished the CA clear-
ce, and the limitations were imposed pending com-
tion. However, the pilots at the CFE criticised these
itations and Boscombe Down did not provide any
port.

The Wing Leader at Waterbeach made his first
ght in the aircraft and after landing was very enthu-
stic, saying it was an absolutely marvellous aircraft
congratulated Supermarine. However, after two
eks with the criticism and lack of support from the
ntral Fighter Establishment (CFE) and Boscombe
wn, no one had a good word for the Swift. The
or serviceability of the aircraft at squadron level did
le to encourage support either.

The Swift FR5, however, was closer to the ultimate
cess with excellent handling and endurance at low
el for tactical fighter reconnaissance at high speed.

The Swift F7 with greater wingspan and armed
h the early Fairey Fireflash missiles, was a very
ent aircraft capable of providing a confirmed kill
every sortie. A trials squadron of 12 aircraft was
med at RAF Valley in North Wales. The overall
ger aircraft was powered by a 100 Series Avon
gine with larger diameter reheat giving an excellent
formance. Reliability was also high and the aircraft
s popular with the pilots, for its good manoeuvra-
ity. The commanding officer of the trials squadron
isted on having squadron fighter pilots, not test
ots, in his unit in order (he said) to get the best
ults from the aircraft and not to find fault. Thanks
this approach, the Swift F7 proved to be a good
ssile platform up to its maximum level speed of
ut Mach 0.93, and was deemed capable of making
erceptions of Mach 0.85 targets at 47,000ft – well

beyond the capability of the threat at the time – but it
was not put into production.

Two Swift F7s (WK275 and WK308) were fitted
with slab all-flying tails, non-linear gearing and datum
shift trimming. This allowed the aircraft to pull up to
5g supersonically and contributed to the Scimitar longitudinal control design, reducing significant development problems and providing outstanding longitudinal
control for that aircraft.

One of Dave Morgan's last tasks on the Swift was
with F7 XF114 on wet runway braking trials at RAF
Upper Heyford. This major Strategic Air Command
(SAC) base was at constant readiness and able to
scramble B-47s at a 15min notice. As a result, if anything blocked the runway when an alert sounded, even
a practice, any obstruction including an aircraft would
be cleared off by a bulldozer. During these braking
trials, the inevitable happened, and a tyre burst during
a braking run down the wetted runway. The rescue
services appeared in ever increasing numbers headed
by the Supermarine ground support truck, which in its
headlong rush had violated a security boundary. The
punctured wheel was removed and replaced by a slave
wheel in 15min and the Swift towed safely away
before the next alert. This particular aircraft survived
to be restored to flying condition at Bournemouth Airport where it is still in the workshops at the time of
writing.

Dave Morgan had little to do with the Supermarine
508 and 529. He says that the full flight envelope was
soon achieved up to 50,000ft, but it had a low critical
Mach number, and snaked during flight. Following the
incident when the undercarriage doors came down in
flight, and control was lost, flutter of the ailerons was
confirmed visually during an air display at Lee-on-
Solent.

The Type 525 was flown occasionally by Dave
Morgan, but it was not a very satisfying aircraft,
although Mike Lithgow was able to present it well at
Farnborough. The aircraft only had a short life, being
lost in a spin and the pilot ejected too late to survive.

When the Scimitar was ready for flight-testing, the
development centre was moved from Chilbolton to the
Vickers Flight Test Centre at Wisley in Surrey. Production aircraft continued to be built at South
Marston. Direct real time telemetry was used for the
first time, especially during spinning trials, with a pilot
monitoring the result on the ground.

The Scimitar was a large aircraft with a maximum
take-off weight of around 41,000lb. It could carry four
1,000lb bombs, or a 2,000lb bomb under one wing and
a large fuel tank under the other and still pull 6g. The
aircraft could release a 2,000lb bomb in a toss bombing LABS manoeuvre and still remain in accurate control with the tank remaining under the other wing. In
the LABS manoeuvre the aircraft would pull up at 4g
at 600kts, the pitch angle at which the bomb would
release, being automatically preset.

Dave was responsible for the weapons and engineering development of the Scimitar, an aircraft which he found a delight to fly, particularly with its full powered controls; as Allan Clifton, then Chief Designer said, '270 men on each aileron and 540 on the tail.'

The first prototype was fitted with slotted flaps, but the second had blown flaps as planned for the production aircraft. With blown flaps, extra lift was generated and the loss of thrust due to bleed required, increased the engine rpm giving excellent control on the approach. To assist on landing, an angle of attack system was fitted, and it was sufficient to follow this and ignore the speed. A simple head-up display indicated by a circle and two arrows whether the angle was high, low or correct. In addition, an audio signal in the earphones gave a constant tone if a correct approach was being flown.

For spinning trials, eight channels of telemetry giving altitude, airspeed, control angles, yaw, roll and pitch together, with a two-way R/T link were provided for a pilot/test observer on the ground. This information was all recorded which dispensed with the need for a chase aircraft. Because of the possibility of pilot disorientation and the critical effect of aileron on spin recovery, roll direction lights were fitted at eye level in the cockpit.

The recommended recovery action was the well-known one of full opposite rudder followed by stick forward and centred until all rotation ceased, as the result of Swift spinning and model tests at RAE. After the first spin this was effective but on the second, after stopping momentarily, rotation started again apparently against full opposite rudder. Within less than a further turn the rate had increased so all controls were released and aileron applied in the direction of the roll indicated by the light, and the spin stopped at once.

Analysis of the records and discussions with RAE at Bedford confirmed that on recovery from the erect spin the aircraft had begun to transfer into an inverted spin; in these circumstances, the roll continues to be i the same direction but the yaw, following the rudde develops in the opposite direction. In either case th application of aileron into the direction of roll wi stop the spin, hence the value of the roll lights.

The occurrence was induced by the 'classical recovery action and Dave found it could be repeate almost at will. But to make life simple for the cus tomer he established that the best way to begi a spin recovery was to let go of everything; if the spi was not fully developed it would stop. If it did no one just took a moment to establish the direction fro the turn needle of the turn and slip indicator an applied opposite rudder.

The Scimitar was a good strong aircraft which i service had no limitation; it could provide all the g an rate of roll a pilot wanted. It was designed for Mac 1.1 at sea level which is 760kts IAS, although onl 700kts was ever achieved. A steep dive was require as the maximum level speed on the deck was abo 630kts, so it was unbreakable. From the operation point of view the pilot had a reasonable workload an was helped in navigation by a basic doppler system The aircraft could act as a tanker so a buddy in-fligl refuelling operation gave it a good radius of actio With four 1,000lb bombs fitted it was cleared to 6 and full aileron operation, so with multiple bom racks it could easily have carried 10,000lb for airfie operations but this, together with the two-seater an thin-wing supersonic versions, were never produce There were other aircraft to do those jobs eventuall but Dave doubts whether they were ever as nice to fl

9

Future Projects

was the advanced weapons system work undertaken by the Supermarine design office which not only contributed strongly to the TSR-2, but also gave Vickers Weybridge a reasonable share with English Electric Preston in the overall programme.

The two main projects to be studied at Hursley Park, before the design office was closed in 1958, were the Types 559 and 571. These programmes were conceived as fully integrated weapons system fighters. The Type 559 was designed to satisfy Operational Requirement 329 in competition with the Saunders Roe P177 mixed powerplant jet/rocket fighter and the Avro 720.

Specification F155T issued in January 1955 required an aircraft capable of destroying targets flying up to Mach 2 at altitudes of 60,000ft, and by using a booster rocket to fly at Mach 2.3 at up to 92,000ft. The perceived threat was high-flying nuclear bombers and the requirement called for a two-seat radar-equipped fighter armed with four air-to-air missiles. Because of the demanding performance, a pair of de Havilland Gyron PS26/1 turbojets mounted one above the other were the conventional powerplants, boosted by reheat and two de Havilland Spectre rocket motors with a fuel duration of 45secs.

The aircraft had a deep fuselage with the air intake under the cockpit and a long nose housing the radar. Canard all-moving foreplanes were proposed giving an improved lift co-efficient. To avoid any vortices which may have been caused by the foreplane, the traditional fuselage-mounted fin and rudder were replaced by wingtip-mounted vertical end plates. The foreplanes were delta-shaped with clipped wingtips, while the main wing had a modest sweepback. Integral fuel tanks in the wings contained up to 960gal, giving an endurance of about 32min. The high operating speeds and altitudes brought problems both in kinetic heating of the skin and solar heating through the canopy which had to be overcome by air conditioning.

To cope with the extremes of the flight envelope a fully automatic control and guidance system would be required, but due to the time it would take to develop such a system, provision was allowed for from the beginning of the programme with a gradual integration of the new systems as the flight development progressed. This would at least avoid delaying the programme unduly and allow the aerodynamic testing to continue. The automatic systems were to control the

aircraft from take-off to touchdown, including mid-course guidance and air interception. Armament was to be the infra-red heat seeking de Havilland Firestreak or Vickers Red Dean semi-active homing missiles. All this development was in the infancy of micro-electronics, digital control and fly-by-wire, and was therefore in an area of very high technological risk.

The Type 559 appeared to stand a good chance of being selected for development for the F155T requirement, but all contestants lost out when the infamous Defence White Paper was published in 1957, cancelling all future development of manned fighters, in favour of ground-to-air missile systems, which at that time were not even defined. The English Electric Lightning survived as an interceptor, and one other requirement for what was basically a Canberra replacement was still needed. This was for an advanced tactical-strike-reconnaissance low level aircraft, the opposite to Type 559 requirement.

This specification was covered by General Operational Requirement GOR339, the main parameters being as follows: a low level tactical-strike aircraft; a medium level bomber; and an all-weather round-the-clock reconnaissance aircraft with a full photographic capability. This requirement was eventually to lead to the TSR-2 produced jointly by Vickers-Armstrong Aircraft and the English Electric Company. These two companies soon became part of the British Aircraft Corporation, together with other organisations, later to be nationalised as part of British Aerospace.

The Supermarine design team made two submissions to GOR339 covered by the Type 571, one a single-engined 40,000lb all-up weight, and the other a twin-engined 81,000lb all-up weight aircraft. Although the requirement called for a twin-engined aircraft, the Supermarine design team favoured the lower weight single-engined project. Their reasoning was that powerplant unreliability was more likely to be caused by ancillaries rather than the basic engine, and therefore by providing duplication of the engine systems, a great deal could be saved in terms of the cost of developing and operating the aircraft. The engines specified were either one or two Rolls-Royce RB142 turbojets with reheat. The larger Type 571 was very similar in overall layout to the eventual TSR-2.

The aircraft was recognised as being part of an overall integrated weapons system, capable of ultra-

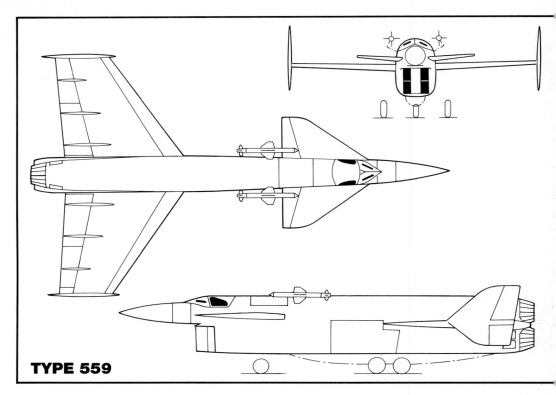

TYPE 559

TYPE 571 (40,000lb)

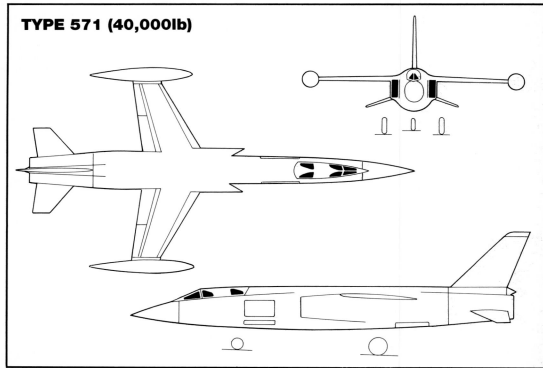

TYPE 571 (81,000lb)

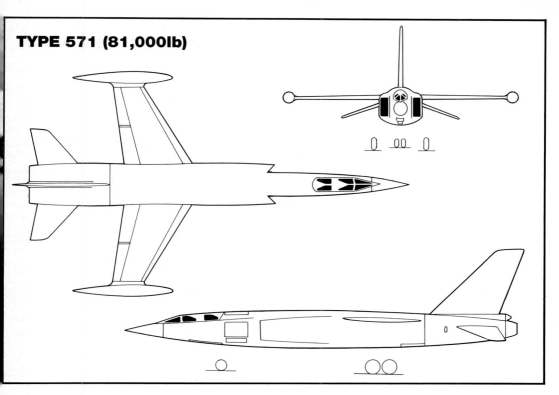

low level clearance operations over hostile territory. Navigation and target identification would include inertial guidance, Doppler distance with moving map, sideways and forward looking radar and automatic weapons delivery. The early development of digital avionics and computing, as compared with the earlier more bulky and less reliable analogue systems, allowed for a drastic reduction in the overall weight and size of the new miniaturised and more reliable equipment. These design principles proved to be of direct benefit to the later development of the TSR-2.

Although the simpler and smaller Type 571 would have followed well the Scimitar down the South Marston production lines, it was the more complex and expensive twin-engined version which formed the basis of the highly political and costly TSR-2, which was abandoned by the British Government just as it was beginning to prove its worth.

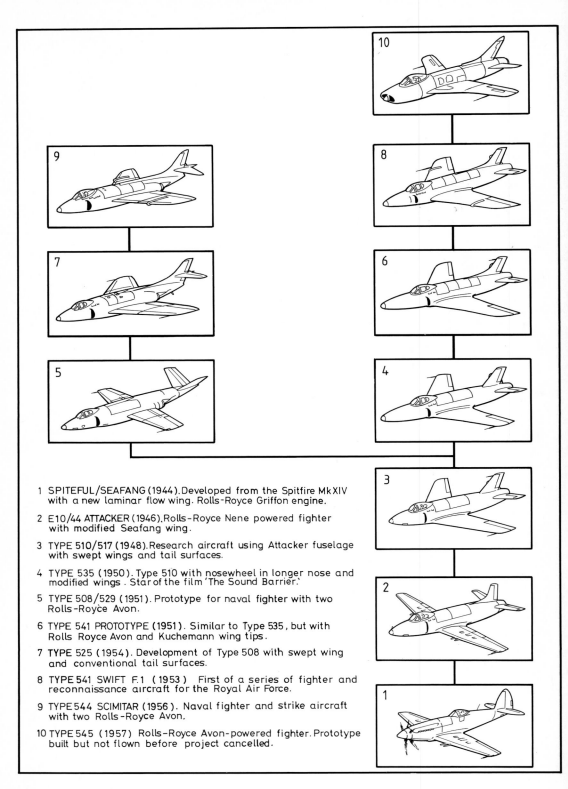

1 SPITEFUL/SEAFANG (1944). Developed from the Spitfire Mk XIV with a new laminar flow wing. Rolls-Royce Griffon engine.

2 E10/44 ATTACKER (1946). Rolls-Royce Nene powered fighter with modified Seafang wing.

3 TYPE 510/517 (1948). Research aircraft using Attacker fuselage with swept wings and tail surfaces.

4 TYPE 535 (1950). Type 510 with nosewheel in longer nose and modified wings. Star of the film 'The Sound Barrier.'

5 TYPE 508/529 (1951). Prototype for naval fighter with two Rolls-Royce Avon.

6 TYPE 541 PROTOTYPE (1951). Similar to Type 535, but with Rolls Royce Avon and Kuchemann wing tips.

7 TYPE 525 (1954). Development of Type 508 with swept wing and conventional tail surfaces.

8 TYPE 541 SWIFT F.1 (1953) First of a series of fighter and reconnaissance aircraft for the Royal Air Force.

9 TYPE 544 SCIMITAR (1956). Naval fighter and strike aircraft with two Rolls-Royce Avon.

10 TYPE 545 (1957) Rolls-Royce Avon-powered fighter. Prototype built but not flown before project cancelled.

Appendix I
Attacker Specifications, Production and Service

Specification

Single-seat, carrier-borne naval fighter of all-metal stressed-skin construction, manufactured by the Supermarine Division of Vickers-Armstrong Ltd, South Marston, Swindon, Wilts.

Powerplant
One 5,100lb thrust Rolls-Royce Nene 3

Dimensions
Wingspan:	36ft 11in
Length:	37ft 6in
Height:	9ft 11in
Wing area:	226sqft

Weights
Empty:	8,434lb
Loaded:	11,500lb

Performance:
Maximum Speed:	590mph at sea level
	538mph at 30,000ft
Climb:	6,350ft/min at sea level
	6.6min to 30,000ft
Service Ceiling:	45,000ft
Range:	590 miles or 1,190 miles with ventral tank

Armament:
Four 20mm cannons mounted in the wings
FB1 also capable of carrying 8 x 60lb/RP or 2 x 1,000lb bombs under the wings

---

Production
Prototypes:	TS409, TS413, and TS416	*3*
F1:	WA469-498, WA505-528	*54*
FB1:	WA529-534	*6*
FB2:	WK319-342, WP275-304, WT851, WZ273-302	*85*

Units

702 Sqn	F1s arrived at Culdrose 3/52. Became Squadron 26/08/52
703 Sqn	F1s at Ford 07–08/51, FB1 1–04/52, FB2 04–08/55, later holding units for 827 Sqn
718 Sqn	Reformed Stretton 25/04/55 to train 1831 Sqn then Honiley 07/55 to train 1833 Sqn, disbanded 31/12/55
700 Sqn	Reformed at Ford 18/08/55 for trials, replacing 703, 771 and 787 Squadrons from 01/56
736 Sqn	Reformed at Culdrose 26/08/52 as Advanced Jet Flying School, moving to Lossiemouth 11/53 and Attackers replaced 08/54
767 Sqn	Equipped with Attackers at Stretton 02/53 for Deck Landing Control Officer training, disbanded 31/03/55
787 Sqn	Trials unit at West Raynham using Attackers from 01/51–09/54
800 Sqn	Reformed at Ford 21/08/51 with 8 x F1s, increasing to 12 x FB2s 12/52 when 890 Sqn disbanded. 800 Sqn disbanded at Ford 01/06/54
803 Sqn	Reformed at Ford 26/11/52 with 8 x F1s, aboard HMS *Eagle*, increased to 12 x FB2s 12/52, replaced by Sea Hawks 08/54
890 Sqn	Reformed at Ford 30/01/52 and commissioned with 8 x F1s, 22/04/52 to provide pilots for 800 and 803 Sqns. Disbanded 03/12/52
1831 Sqn	RNVR Re-equipped at Stretton 05/55 with 7 x FB2s and disbanded 10/03/57 in defence cuts
1832 Sqn	RNVR Re-equipped at Benson 08/55 with 8 x FB2s. Attackers gone by end 1956 and disbanded 10/03/57
1833 Sqn	RNVR Re-equipped at Bramcote 10/55 with 7 x FB2s, but moved jet operations to Honiley. Disbanded 10/03/57
Airwork	Based at St Davids with Attackers 12/55–01/57
FRU Hurn	Used Attackers 10/55–02/57

Appendix II
Swift Specifications, Production and Service

Specification

Single-seat interceptor day-fighter or fighter-recon-naissance of all-metal stressed-skin construction, man-ufactured by the Supermarine Division of Vickers-Armstrong Ltd, South Marston, Swindon, Wilts.

Powerplant

One 7,500lb thrust Rolls-Royce Avon RA7 (F1 and F2)
One 7,500lb thrust Rolls-Royce Avon RA7R (F3 and F4)
One 7,175lb thrust Rolls-Royce Avon 114 (F5) 9,450lb with reheat
One 9,950lb thrust Rolls-Royce Avon 116 (F7)

	F1	F2	FR5	F7
Dimensions				
Wingspan:	32ft 4.0in	32ft 4.0in	32ft 4in	35ft
Length:	41ft 5.5in	41ft 5.5in	42ft 3in	43ft 9in
Height:	13ft 6.0in	13ft 6.0in	13ft 6in	13ft 6in
Wing Area:	306sq ft	321sq ft	328sq ft	348sq ft
Weights				
Empty:	11,892lb	13,136lb	13,435lb	13,735lb
Loaded:	15,800lb	19,764lb	21,673lb	21,400lb
Performance				
Max Speed at Sea Level:				
	660mph	709mph	713mph	700mph
Initial Climb:	12,300ft/min	14,540ft/min	14,660ft/min	–
Service Ceiling:	45,500ft	39,000ft	45,800ft	41,600ft
Range:	730 miles	493 miles	630 miles	864 miles
Armament				
	2 x 20mm cannon	4 x 20mm cannon	–	2 x Fireflash

Production

Prototypes:	Type 510 VV106, Type 535 VV119, Type 541 WJ960, WJ965	*4*
F1	WK194-213	*20*
F2	WK214-221, WK239-246	*16*
F3	WK247-271	*25*
F4	WK272-280 (many converted to FR5)	*9*
FR5	WK281, WK287-315, WN124 XE 903-930, XD 948-977 (XD 978-988 cancelled)	*89*
F7	XF113-124 (XF125-258 with gaps, cancelled)	*12*
F7	XF774, XF778	*2*

Units

56 Sqn F1s 02/54–05/55 at Waterbeach and F2s 1954 – 05/59

2 Sqn FR5s 03/56–04/61 at Geilenkirchen and Jever

79 Sqn FR5 1956–01/01/61 at Guterslöh

4 Sqn FR5 01/61 at Guterslöh

1 GWDS F7 04/57–11/58 at Valley

Appendix III
Scimitar Specification, Production and Service

Specification

Single-seat, carrier-borne medium to high level interceptor, fighter-reconnaissance or low-level nuclear strike aircraft, of all-metal stressed-skin construction, manufactured by the Supermarine Division of Vickers-Armstrong Ltd, South Marston, Swindon, Wilts.

Powerplant
Two 11,250lb thrust Rolls-Royce Avon 202

Dimensions
Wingspan:	37ft 2in
Length:	55ft 4in
Height:	15ft 3in
Wing Area:	484.9sq ft

Weights
Empty:	23,962lb
Loaded:	34,200lb

Performance
Max Speed:	710mph at 10,000 ft
Climb:	12,000ft/min
Service Ceiling:	46,000ft
Range:	1,422 miles at 35,000ft

Armament
Four 30mm cannon and 4 x 1,000lb bombs, or 4 Bullpup air-to-ground missiles, or 4 Sidewinder air-to-air missiles

Production

Prototypes:	Type 508 VX133, Type 529 VX136, Type 525 VX138	*3*
	N113 WT854, WT859, WW134	*3*
F1:	XD212–250, XD264–282, XD316–333 (XD334–357 cancelled)	*76*

Units

700X Sqn	08/57–06/58 at Ford
736 Sqn	06/59–26/03/65 at Lossiemouth for operational training
764 Sqn	1959 at Lossiemouth for Air Weapons training
800 Sqn	01/07/59 at Lossiemouth and *Ark Royal* until 25/02/64 into 803 Sqn
803 Sqn	03/06/58 at Lossiemouth and *Victorious*, *Hermes* and *Ark Royal* until disbandment 01/10/66
804 Sqn	01/03/60 at Lossiemouth and *Hermes*, disbanded 15/09/61
807 Sqn	01/10/58 at Lossiemouth, *Ark Royal* and *Centaur*, disbanded 15/05/62
FRU	12/65–12/70 at Hurn

Appendix IV
Surviving Supermarine Jet Fighters

Attacker F1
WA473 ex-736, 702 and 800 Sqns — FAA Museum, Yeovilton

Supermarine 517
VV 106 — RAF Museum, Cosford

Supermarine 535
VV119 cockpit section only – Lincs Aviation Society, East Kirkby

Swift
F4 WK198 fuselage only — NE Aircraft Museum, Sunderland
F4 WK275 — Lion Motors, Upper Hill
FR5 WK277 ex– 2 Sqn — Newark Air Museum
FR5 WK281 ex–79 Sqn — RAF Museum, Hendon
F7 XF113 nose only — Bath
F7 XF114 under restoration to fly — Jet Heritage, Bournemouth

Supermarine 544
WT859 fuselage in poor condition — PEE Foulness

Scimitars
XD317 ex-FRU, RAE, 800, 736, 807 Sqns— FAA Museum, Yeovilton (store)
XD332 ex-764B, 736, 807, 804 Sqns — Flambards Museum, Helston

XD215, XD219, XD235, XD244, XD267, XD322 fuselage only — PEE Foulness
XD228 and XD231 — Calvert's Scrapyard, Thirsk
XD241 and XD243 — PEE Pendine
XD220 Intrepid Air-Sea-Space Museum, New York, USA

Below:
Attacker F1, WA473, was the only one of the type to escape scrapping at Abbotsinch. It is now the sole survivor, preserved at the FAA Museum at Yeovilton.
M. J. F. Bowyer

Top right:
Swift FR5, WK277:N of No 2 Squadron, RAF is preserved at the Newark Air Museum and seen here in April 1976. *P. J. Birtles*

Centre right:
Swift FR5, WK281:S of No 79 Squadron, RAF, was displayed at the Royal Review of the RAF at Abingdon in June 1968, having been preserved at Finningley, and can now be seen at the RAF Museum, Hendon.
P. J. Birtles

Bottom right:
Scimitar F1, XD317:112/R of 800 Squadron, FAA, is preserved by the FAA Museum, Yeovilton, and is seen here in September 1970. *P. J. Birtles*

Type 508 VX133 and Type 535 XV119 are pictured flying together towards Farnborough for display in the 1951 show. *Vickers*